TESTIMONY

TESTIMONY

Talking Ourselves into Being Christian

Thomas G. Long

JOSSEY-BASS
A Wiley Imprint
www.josseybass.com

Published by Jossey-Bass
A Wiley Imprint
989 Market Street, San Francisco, CA 94103-1741   www.josseybass.com

Jossey-Bass books and products are available through most bookstores. To contact
Jossey-Bass directly call our Customer Care Department within the U.S.
at 800-956-7739, outside the U.S. at 317-572-3986, or fax 317-572-4002.

Jossey-Bass also publishes its books in a variety of electronic formats.
Some content that appears in print may not be available in electronic books.

Credits are on page 179.

Library of Congress Cataloging-in-Publication Data
Long, Thomas G., date.
Testimony: talking ourselves into being Christian / Thomas G. Long.—1st ed.
p. cm.—(The practices of faith series)
Includes bibliographical references (p.) and index.
ISBN 0-7879-6832-3 (alk. paper)
1. Witness bearing (Christianity) I. Title. II. Series.
BV4520.L56 2004
248'.5—dc22
2004005675

Printed in the United States of America
FIRST EDITION

HB Printing   10 9 8 7 6 5 4 3 2

The Practices of Faith Series
Dorothy C. Bass, Series Editor

For Don and Peg Bracken,
who are faithful witnesses

Contents

Editor's Foreword

Talk is cheap, or so they say. Listen in on daily life, and it's hard to disagree. We live in the midst of a vast ocean of talk. The resulting flood of words is not always cheap in an economic sense, because much of it is devoted to advertising, but it can cheapen our lives in a more important way when it diminishes the value of the things that matter most. Much of what people need to talk to one another about—love, anger, forgiveness, promise—is not only beyond price but also, often, beyond words. And yet we keep on talking, using language as we interpret our world and try to connect with one another. Doing so, we find again and again that the kind of talk we most need can be quite costly. To our surprise, however, the right words sometimes come to our lips, or to our ears, as a gift.

In *Testimony: Talking Ourselves into Being Christian*, Thomas Long invites readers into a conversation on how to talk about what matters most. In particular, he helps us to consider how to talk with integrity about God during our everyday lives at home, at work, or in the public square. Within a society shared by people of many faiths or none, such talk can seem difficult, even dangerous—especially because some of those who talk most loudly about God appear to view many of their fellow human beings with disdain. Indeed, many well-intentioned people wonder whether it is ever possible to talk about religious beliefs without becoming arrogant—or dying of embarrassment.

Thomas Long is honest regarding the complexities of speaking about faith within the current social and cultural context, but he does not allow these complexities to halt the search for honest testimony. The worship and daily ways of Christian communities across the ages, rightly understood, hold a good deal of wisdom for a contemporary culture that is awash in cheap talk. Critical yet loving attention to the

Christian practice of testimony, Long shows, can help us speak of God with integrity within the real contexts of our daily lives. But that is not all. This book also claims that *talking* faithfully is one important aspect of *living* faithfully.

One of the most insightful Christians to ponder how talk about God shapes one's walk in the world was Augustine of Hippo, who earned his living teaching Roman citizens the art of persuasive speech before becoming a Christian and eventually a bishop. Words, Augustine observed as he watched fourth-century children learn to speak, are "precious cups of meaning" that allow human beings to enter into community. He also knew from experience, however, that words can become "weapons" when they emerge from the mouths of those who seek to dominate rather than to love and serve.[1]

Thomas Long also makes his living teaching others to speak persuasively, though in a different context. As a professor in a divinity school, he helps Christian ministers discover words of clarity and vigor and grace with which to speak to their communities about God's active presence for the life of the world. In this book Long takes a wider view, offering his love of God and his gift of strong and merciful speech to a larger group of talkers. Here he becomes the teacher of all who would offer their testimony not in pulpits but in offices, stores, bedrooms, ballparks, and every other place of conversation.

In all these settings, people yearn for talk about God that comes as an invitation to share a precious cup of meaning, for talk about God that is not used as a weapon. A supple, sturdy practice that addresses these yearnings comes into view in this book. I am delighted to add it to the Practices of Faith Series, which offers resources drawn from the deep wells of Christian belief and experience to those who long to live with integrity in the rapidly changing world of the twenty-first century. *Testimony* will provide Christian readers fresh perspectives and renewed hope as they speak the familiar words of faith; it also will offer challenge and wisdom to spiritual seekers who long to hear the truth spoken in love.

As you explore these pages and consider how you may grow as one who offers faithful testimony within your own daily life, I encourage you to find companions with whom to discuss, pray about, and live this practice. To assist you in this endeavor, *A Guide for Conversation, Learning, and Growth,* based on this book, is available at www. practicingourfaith.org.

June 2004   DOROTHY C. BASS
Valparaiso, Indiana   Editor, Practices of Faith Series

Acknowledgments

There are, according to the author Ben Cheever, at least two things wrong with acknowledgments in books. The first is that there is always an air of implied hubris about them; their very existence seems to presume that something wonderful has been accomplished. The second is that acknowledgments are altogether too cheerful. "Every woman cherishes her husband, every writer, his publisher," Cheever complains. "The children, if mentioned, seem to have spent years tiptoeing around in felt slippers, presenting trays of tea and toast to the invalid genius. Who are these people? Acknowledgments often leave me with the impression that I've been lied to."[1]

As if that were not enough, the critic David Oshinsky piles on a third problem, namely, that most acknowledgments simply list too many names. In a book he reviewed recently, Oshinsky claimed that if even half of the people named in the acknowledgments purchased the book, it would be a runaway best-seller.[2]

So here come the acknowledgments, but I believe that I can honestly plead innocent of hubris. I am all too keenly aware that most of the ideas in this book, and all of the good ones, have been borrowed from others, to whom I am indebted. As for the charges of excessive cheer and the listing of too many names, the reader will have to judge that. I am, in fact, cheerfully grateful for those people whose support and stimulation I needed as I wrote, and there are a lot of them.

I will never forget a comment that one of my teachers, the great Lutheran preacher and professor Edmund Steimle, made about preaching. Facing a roomful of clergy and betting that most of them fancied themselves to be—ahem—scintillating and accomplished preachers, Steimle growled, "A good sermon is not a beautiful package with a pretty bow tied by the preacher. A good sermon is like the rings on the surface of a lake when the preacher has gone down in deep water."

I do know, having dived into the murky pool of Christian testimony, that I have been in deep water, and I also am quite aware that I have often been way over my head here. My best hope, then, is that in this book you can see the rings on the water where I took the plunge.

And I would like to thank some of the people who pushed me into the lake.

Dorothy Bass is a great friend and an intellectual companion whose fine theological sensibilities and broad knowledge of the language of practices has greatly shaped my own thought. Dorothy is the director of the Valparaiso Project on the Education and Formation of People in Faith, which has given needed and appreciated support for the writing of the manuscript.

The publisher Jossey-Bass has a treasure in editor Sheryl Fullerton, who gave good direction to the work. My friends Barbara Brown Taylor, Patrick Willson, Ted Wardlaw, Joanna Adams, William Willimon, Fred Craddock, William J. Boyd, and Tom Lynch are all lovers of words, and just watching them put words to work so well encouraged me to keep at this. My dearest friend, Craig Dykstra, could have done a better job on this book than I, but he is kind enough to share his ideas unselfishly and friend enough to be gladdened when he sees but pale reflections of them here and there in these pages. My research assistant, Alex Tracy, who reads Seneca and Plato when he's not tracking down footnotes, is to be thanked not only for working the whisk broom behind my research but also for making many wonderful suggestions.

And finally, I want to thank my wife and my true companion, Kim, for all she does to make our life together a joyful place.

T.G.L.

If I have achieved anything in my life, it is because I have not been embarrassed to talk about God.

—Dorothy Day, founder, Catholic Workers Movement

The words with which we praise God shape the world in which we shall live.

—Walter Brueggemann, Old Testament scholar

TESTIMONY

Part One

THE HUNGER FOR AUTHENTIC GOD TALK

Chapter 1

TALKING OURSELVES INTO BEING CHRISTIAN

A shrewd New Yorker, a person of faith, once wryly noted, "At fashionable dinner parties in this town, you can talk about anything. You can talk about politics, you can talk about sex, you can talk about money, you can talk about anything you want. But if you mention God more than once, you probably won't be invited back."

This book is about an important but potentially uncomfortable topic: how ordinary Christians talk about God and faith when we are not in church. It is about how we put our faith into words when we are at places like dinner parties and neighborhood meetings, how we express our faith when we are talking to our families, with people at work, in social gatherings with our friends, and out in the community. Talking about God outside of church is a potentially uncomfortable topic because it places many Christians in a bind. On the one hand, we know that our faith touches everything about life. It affects our relationships, our politics, the way we spend our money and spend our time. How strange if our faith did not show up in our everyday talk. On the other hand, everybody knows that God and religion, like sex and money, are touchy matters, and speaking about faith in public always runs the risk of offense or even social rejection. Few people want to wear their religion on their sleeves—or their T-shirts—and run the risk of sounding like a "Jesus freak" or committing a social *faux pas*. As the New Yorker said, "If you mention God more than once, you probably won't be invited back."

No wonder many of us choose to be quiet and private about our faith, even though we know that our faith is not just a quietly private matter. We can get through the day very well, thank you, without using God talk. We can coach a soccer team, take a legal deposition, chat with a neighbor, teach a math class, volunteer at a homeless shelter, write an insurance policy, or ring up a sale without thrusting our faith into the equation, at least in words—so why bring it up and run the risk of putting somebody off and being embarrassed? We are not even sure that we are the ones to speak or that we would know what to say anyway.

In Lynna Williams's touching and hilarious short story "Personal Testimony," a twelve-year-old minister's daughter at a Southern Baptist summer camp earns hundreds of dollars running "a ghost-writing service for Jesus," composing for the other campers the personal testimonies of conversion and repentance they are expected to give, amid tears and hallelujahs, at evening worship each night of camp.[1] The story plays off the anxiety of many Christians that we lack the words to describe our faith in public, that we need somebody else to create the language. Better leave that to the professional talkers, the preachers and the evangelists. We reassure ourselves that our reticence is for the best by quoting Edgar Guest's poem: "I'd rather see a sermon than hear one any day."[2] Or as the comedian Flip Wilson used to reply when asked about his religious preference: "I'm a Jehovah's Bystander. They wanted me to become a Jehovah's Witness, but I don't want to get involved."

TO TELL THE TRUTH

Even though this book is about putting our faith into words out in streets and avenues of everyday life, I hasten to add that it is not a book about techniques of what some people call "personal witnessing" or "evangelism." There is a place for books on that theme, but sometimes the underlying assumption of such books is that the only reason why a Christian would want to speak publicly about faith is to convert other people, to persuade them to become Christians too. But evangelism (at least as traditionally understood) is not the only reason, indeed not even the deepest reason, why Christians bring their faith to speech. At the most profound level, Christians talk about faith because it is a truly human act to want to tell the truth.

Periodically, some long-suppressed story will erupt onto the front page of the newspaper, an old scandal, perhaps, or a bad memory the local authorities buried, and almost inevitably someone will be quoted saying, to the effect, "The story had to be told. It just had to be told." It is as if there is a drive within us to get the truth out, to tell the whole story. To be sure, human beings tell lies every day—big lies, hurtful lies, polite lies, and little sneaky lies—but underneath the skin there is a restless discomfort with lying (which is the principle behind the lie detector). On the surface, we often think that we need to lie, that lies can get us out of trouble and make life somehow better, but underneath we desperately want to tell the truth, the whole truth, and nothing but the truth. It is a human thing to do.

Christians believe that we cannot tell the truth, not the whole truth, without talking about God, and if we cannot tell the whole truth, we cannot be fully alive as human beings. Say we are standing on the shore of a lake at the close of day, watching the orange orb of the sun sink into the water, setting the sky on fire in a display of color and radiance. Someone on the shore may remark that such sunsets are the product of light refraction and atmospheric dust. That's true, of course, but it isn't the whole truth. Others may contribute various facts about this sunset—duration, color spectrum, intensity—but these would still not add up to the whole truth. If we stay on the shore long enough and watch the playful beauty of creation on display before our very eyes, eventually someone will say something like "The heavens declare the glory of God." Why would someone say a thing like that? Because human beings finally want to tell the whole truth.

Imagine a society in which music were illegal. In this society, it would be against the law to sing, to listen to music, to harbor a musician in one's home, or even to quote the lyrics of a song. Undoubtedly, there would soon be a revolution in such a society, because a law against music would be more than just an unwelcome irritation; it would be a moral outrage, a crime against the human spirit. Human beings don't just enjoy music; we need music to be human, and we cannot be fully human if we cannot make music. In the same way, Christians know that we cannot be fully human without speaking the truth about life and about ourselves, which is grounded in the truth about God. Even if every person in the world were already a Christian, we would still need to talk about God in the same way that a mariner needs to talk about the sea. We would need to talk about God to be truthful, to be whole, for life to be full.

A common misunderstanding is to think that talking about faith means getting our belief system all worked out in advance before we open our mouths. When we speak about our faith, we intuitively think that what we are doing is finding the language to say what we already know we believe. That is, we get our beliefs formulated in our minds and hearts, and then we search for just the right words to capture what is already fixed and established. But things are actually more complex than this. We don't just say things we already believe. To the contrary, saying things out loud is a part of how we come to believe. We talk our way *toward* belief, talk our way from tentative belief through doubt to firmer belief, talk our way toward believing more fully, more clearly, and more deeply. Putting things into words is one of the ways we acquire knowledge, passion, and conviction. For example, when two people love each other, they naturally speak to each other of their love. But as they whisper love's words to each other deep into the night, they are not simply expressing their love; they are *discovering* their love, even *creating* their love, its power, its prospects, its limits. Putting their love for each other into words gives it a content, a shape, a definition, a depth, and a future it did not have when it was just a formless emotion surging wildly in their hearts.

So it is that trying to put our faith into words is a part of discovering what we know about God, believe about God, and trust about God. Sometimes seminary students struggling to compose their first sermons will exclaim in frustration, "I know what I believe. I just can't *say* it!" This is understandable, but in some ways, just the reverse is true. Unless you can say it, you don't really believe it. The most effective Bible study groups, for example, allow for a free flow of honest conversation, questioning, probing, exploration, and even skepticism, because it is the experience of such groups that putting ideas into words in dialogue with others is an important aspect of how we come to know and believe the wisdom of the Scripture. When we talk about our faith, we are not merely expressing our beliefs; we are coming more fully and clearly to believe. In short, we are always talking ourselves into being Christian.[3]

Most of us are not professional theologians, and for many Christians, almost all talk about God occurs when we are inside the church. This is not surprising, since talking about God inside the church is often a lot easier and much less threatening than talking about God out in the world. Inside the church, in worship, speaking about God and to God comes rather naturally because, after all, that's what we're supposed to be doing, and the hymns and prayers give us the words to say. We sing the doxology, say "amen," read the Scripture, or recite the Apostles' Creed, and we don't have to search for the right words or feel uncomfortable about speaking them. The grooves of what to say and how to say it are already carved into the service of worship and into our memory.

But what about speaking of God in the rest of life? How do we talk about God to our children? Should we allow our faith to find voice when the tensions rise in a business meeting, when a friend comes back from the clinic with a troubling diagnosis, when we are at a PTA meeting discussing school policy, when a neighbor leans over the backyard fence to talk about her kids, or when a guy from down the block drops by with a petition on some community concern? Should we talk about God at a dinner party, even when we run the risk of not being invited back? This is, for many of us, unexplored territory, and the awkwardness of trying to speak faithfully out in the world tends to make us mute. We are unsure how to put our faith into words in nonchurchy places, so we often just say nothing.

GOD CHATTER

If it is true, as I am claiming, that we Christians are often reticent about faith and frequently choose just to keep our mouths closed in public about God, why there is so much evidence to the contrary? Our culture chatters about God incessantly. There is a plenty of God talk out there in the public arena. Politicians talk about God. Televangelists talk about God. Mystics who write best-selling books on spirituality talk about God. People in sports stadiums frantically wave posters with Bible passages. Evangelists pass out "Are You Saved?" tracts door to door. Radio DJs and TV newscasters toss off references to God. Popular movies and supermarket tabloids rattle on about God. Some highway billboards even purport to be messages from God ("Don't make me come down there—God"). Just turn on the radio, read *People* magazine, or ride down Main Street—God talk reverberates everywhere.

We sense, though, that amid all the God chatter and religious white noise there is a serious lack of depth, even what could be called a famine of authentic speech about God. People talk and talk and talk about God, but the language often seems empty. The God words strike the ear with the dull clink of counterfeit coins. What is missing in our culture is not God talk but authentic God talk. When the Bible, describing a particular moment in Israel's history, says, "The word of the Lord was rare in those days" (1 Samuel 3:1), it does not mean that people did not talk about God then. No doubt, people in that time spoke about God as much as ever—in houses of worship, in homes, in the marketplace. It was just that all of their God talk lacked the ring of authenticity. In short, there was a lot of God talk but very little God in it.

What we are running into here is the realization that there are significantly different ways to talk about God. One way—and this characterizes a lot of what passes for religious talk in society—is to say the word *God* but really to mean something else. *God* can be a convenient term to describe a whole host of significant values, deep feelings, and big ideas. *God* is a word that can stand in for such things as political ambition ("with God on our side"), conventional wisdom

("God helps those who help themselves"), accepted morality ("she was a God-fearing woman"), or our own inner urges ("God wants me to prosper"). In such cases, people say *God,* but they mean things that aren't God—important things, perhaps, even things that are sacred to our culture, but not really God.

Consider the recent court tussle over the phrase "one nation, under God," which for decades many schoolchildren have recited every morning as they pledged allegiance to the American flag. A furor erupted when a circuit court panel ruled that this phrase was now illegal to use in public institutions because the naming of God violated the constitutional separation of church and state. The battle lines were drawn. Some people were cheered by the court's ruling, seeing it as a victory for tolerance and inclusiveness, while others, citing the religious roots of the nation, protested angrily that the court had gone too far. Perhaps the most interesting response, voiced in some newspaper editorials and elsewhere, was that even if the phrase "one nation, under God" is a technical breech of the wall between church and state, it is a harmless violation, and it be would be wise for the courts to leave it alone. After all, went the logic, the phrase "one nation, under God" refers to something vague and gaseous, something akin to general American spiritual values, and not to any real deity currently presiding over a religious movement. One commentator observed that, while "under God" sounds religious, it really symbolizes an underlying secular meaning. It is, he said, "ceremonial deism." In short, we may say "under God" in public, but make no mistake, we don't really mean *God.*

Or suppose that a mountain climber standing at the foot of Mount Everest points toward the crest and says, "We'll make it to the top, God willing." Now what does he really mean by "God willing"? Who knows? We would have to ask him to know for certain, but the chances are good that he is not really talking about God or God's will at all, or at least not in a significant way. What he probably means is something like, "We are determined to the best of our ability to climb to the top of Everest, but climbing a mountain like this forces us to face our limits, to admit that much of this is beyond our control." In other words, the explorer means that getting to the top of Everest

Talking Ourselves into Being Christian

depends on such things as determination, the ropes holding, and the climbers not being swept away by an avalanche—in short, an alchemy of pluck and luck, a combination of perseverance, accommodating weather, chance, and good fortune. He says "God willing" because the word *God* is a socially useful term for events that lie beyond human sway.

It is possible to be too cynical about this ceremonial use of God talk. Some of it, to be sure, is throwaway speech, an empty and maybe even destructive use of sacred language for all-too-worldly ends. A more generous hearing, though, will recognize that much of this ceremonial use of faith language reflects a memory, however dim, of God's presence and even a hunger for a renewed encounter with God. As novelist Frederick Buechner once said about the custom of giving theological names to colonial settlements, "New Haven, New Hope, they called them—names that almost bring tears to your eyes if you listen to what they are saying, or once said. Providence, Concord, Salem, which is *shalom,* the peace that passeth all understanding."[4] Providence and Salem are not just the names of our oldest towns; they are the embodiments of our deepest hopes. When people in the culture speak casually and apparently unreflectively about God, this is not simply a matter of nonchalance or a sign of how thoroughly secular society has become; it is also a tacit confession of the need for authentic speech about God. Even "God dammit!" is not just a fierce curse; it is also an attempt to summon a power not possessed by ordinary language, a profane and ironic pointing to the power of sacred speech and of the hunger for an encounter with the living God.

THE RING OF TRUTH

This hunger for an authentic encounter with God in fact points toward another kind of God talk, God talk that takes the presence of the living God seriously and tries to tell the truth about how God is active in our lives. In fact, such talk is not just "about" God; it is also a participation in the very life of God. When a mother says to a worried kindergartener on the opening day of school, "Don't worry.

You'll be fine here. They'll take care of you, and Mommy will come back to get you soon," she is doing far more than merely uttering soothing sentiments. She is using words to evoke a world, a world in which she loves her child and would never abandon him, a world in which her child is a person of inestimable value, a sturdy world in which her child can live confidently. By and through her words, she is summoning to reality the cords of trust she wants her child to hold on to. She is invoking by her speech a world of safety and protection and saying to her child, "This is my word. You can live under its strong branches. You can rely on this. It won't let you down." In the same way, to speak truthfully about God is also to enter into a world, a world in which God is present and can be trusted. To speak about God is to live in that world and to speak out of it. To speak about God is to be in relationship to God, which means that speaking about God is more than speaking *about* God; it is also speaking for, in, with, and to God. Authentic speech about God, therefore, can be said to be a form of prayer.

Authentic God talk is so out of the ordinary, so against the grain of everyday speech, that it often startles us when we hear it. When the first Christian preachers, Peter and John, engaged in their first attempts to speak the gospel, the effect was startling. Peter and John were common people, uneducated and coarse, but when they boldly spoke the truth about Jesus as they had seen and heard it, people were astonished (Acts 4:13).

Many years ago, the Reverend Martin Luther King Sr., the elderly father of the slain civil rights leader, was invited to close the meeting of the Democratic National Convention with a benediction, a prayerful blessing. When the final gavel had fallen on the convention business, a throaty cheer arose from the convention floor, and a celebration broke out among the delegates. They were at the end of a long week of politicking, had just elected a presidential ticket, and were now in a festive, perhaps even riotous, party mood. Balloons were floating to the ceiling of the hall, and the floor was boiling with people high-fiving each other, ripping campaign literature into confetti, shouting greetings, and slapping backs. In an announcement that could barely be heard above the din, "Daddy" King was introduced

Talking Ourselves into Being Christian

and walked to the podium to stand before the noisy, giddily jubilant crowd. It seemed hardly the occasion for God talk, but King stood silently before the delegates until gradually the ripples of movement ceased and people, realizing something was about to happen, turned their attention expectantly to the podium. Slowly King raised his arms and began to speak. "May the Lord bless you and keep you," King intoned, his majestic bass voice making the words ring, and a strange stillness fell over the crowd. "May the Lord make his face to shine upon you, and be gracious to you," King continued, his whole body caught up in the power of this blessing. "May the Lord lift up his countenance upon you, and give you peace." As King spoke, an awestruck reverence fell upon the crowd. All recognized that King was saying something more than a ceremonial word and that what was being said was more important than a presidential ticket, deeper than politics. This was not just the close of a ceremony; this was startling speech, a true blessing from God.

It is not surprising to find that the culture sometimes gets confused and mixes up ceremonial and authentic God talk. In a famous legal and medical case several years ago, a young New Jersey woman, Karen Ann Quinlan, lapsed into a coma after a night of socializing with friends, probably the result of a bad interaction of alcohol and prescription medicine. She was hospitalized and placed on life support. When it became apparent, after many months had passed, that Karen Ann would never recover consciousness, her parents, devout Christians and entrusting their daughter to God, asked for the life support machines to be removed. The hospital refused to honor their request, and the Quinlans were forced to go to court in what was a pioneering case in medical ethics.

In the trial, Joseph Quinlan, Karen Ann's father, petitioned the court to explain why they had requested the removal of life support. For Joseph and his wife, this was a faith decision, and in his testimony, Joseph explained that they were convinced that Karen Ann was beyond earthly hope and that she should be turned over in trust to the Lord's will and to the hope of heaven. Quinlan prayed that the court would recognize this as a deeply religious matter.

The court, however, unaccustomed to such faith language, was confused by it and finally rejected it. The only admissible definitions of "life" and "death," the court told Joseph Quinlan, were those provided by medical authorities. Moreover, the court told Quinlan that what he considered a "religious" issue was not deemed so by the court, which held all authority over what was and was not a religious issue in this case. How did the court finally hear Joseph Quinlan's faith testimony? The court said that Quinlan was obviously "sincere" and that he had given an "expression of personal faith." In other words, the court treated his religious language ceremonially and as merely the traces of a man with good character.[5]

"The only thing worse than being misunderstood," goes the old quip, "is being understood." Indeed, if the judge in the Quinlan case misunderstood Joseph Quinlan's faith testimony and viewed it as benign evidence that Quinlan was a good citizen, sometimes such faith speech is understood all too well. Because authentic talk about God conveys the very presence of God, and God's presence is always challenging and demanding, it is not surprising that public speaking about God sometimes generates resistance or even angry rejection.

In the mid-1970s, when the famed dissident Alexander Solzhenitsyn defected from the Soviet Union to America, there was great rejoicing in American diplomatic circles. What a coup this was, what a comeuppance for the Soviets. "Just wait," warned the Russians, "you'll find out about Solzhenitsyn." In 1978, Harvard University invited Solzhenitsyn, then living in the United States, to deliver the commencement address at its graduation ceremonies. Thousands gathered to hear the famous novelist, undoubtedly expecting Solzhenitsyn to denounce the totalitarian Soviet regime and to celebrate the freedom, tolerance, and prosperity of the West. Instead, Solzhenitsyn caught the crowd off guard with a speech that denounced Western civilization's moral lassitude and spiritual poverty. Solzhenitsyn's speech that day was deeply and thoroughly religious, and some members of the audience even booed as he dared to disrupt the polite commencement exercises with words about God and the life of faith. Solzhenitsyn said,

Talking Ourselves into Being Christian

On the way from the Renaissance to our days we have enriched our experience, but we have lost the concept of a Supreme Complete Entity which used to restrain our passions and our irresponsibility. We have placed too much hope in political and social reforms, only to find out that we were being deprived of our most precious possession: our spiritual life. In the East, it is destroyed by the dealings and machinations of the ruling party. In the West, commercial interests tend to suffocate it. This is the real crisis.[6]

The Russians were right: we found out about Solzhenitsyn, and what we found out was that he is not just a "good man," a nice guy. He is more like an Old Testament prophet, more like an austere and saintly desert monk, and with Solzhenitsyn, as is the case with Jeremiah and with the saints, surely no one needs to remind him that "if you mention God more than once, you probably won't be invited back."

Speaking publicly about our faith, then, is powerful but also perilous. Our words can be a startling blessing to others, but they can also be misunderstood and even booed off the stage. So why would ordinary Christians, who could easily spend a lifetime singing the hymns on Sunday and keeping our mouths shut the rest of the week, want to explore the possibilities for speaking about God out there in the rest of life? Perhaps those old preachers, Peter and John, had the best answer. When the authorities, worried about their words' stirring up the people, ordered them to shut up, Peter and John replied that the authorities would have to judge for themselves whether speaking the gospel was against the law, and then they added, "But we cannot keep from speaking about what we have seen and heard" (Acts 4:19–20).

KNOWING THE WAY

One of the earliest names given to the Christian movement sounds a bit odd: "the Way" (Acts 9:2). Just that, "the Way." When we think about it, though, "the Way" is a very apt name for Christianity because it captures at least two major truths about the faith. First, any group called "the Way" (it can also be translated "the Road") are clearly people who are going somewhere. Ever since God told Abraham to leave his country and family behind and to head out "to a land I will show you" (Genesis 12:1), the people of God have been on the move. If you are a Christian, keep your bags packed and your eye on the highway, because the life of faith is a continual journey. Sometimes this journey is symbolic in the sense that Christians are always changing, growing, and moving along the road toward a deeper faith in God. But often the traveling done by Christians is a quite literal. If there is a settlement down the highway where the gospel has not yet been shared, eventually Christians will put their feet, their boats, their horses, or their cars into motion and go there.

This picture of the Christian faith as a journey, as "the Road," has implications for how we understand this matter of speaking our faith to and with others. The Apostle Paul, quoting the prophet Isaiah, once said of people who speak gospel, "How beautiful are the feet of those who bring good news" (Romans 10:15). Now, one would expect Paul to say, "How beautiful are the *words* of those who bring good news" or "How beautiful are the *faces* of those who speak the gospel" or "How beautiful are the *mouths*" or "How beautiful are the *churches*" or even "How beautiful are the *stained-glass windows.*" But no—how beautiful are the *feet.* This reason for this is that before we can open our mouths to speak some good news from God, we usually have to burn a little shoe leather to journey to the people who need to hear these words of comfort. Whether it is traveling to a hospital ward, entering the family room at the funeral home, going across the street to a neighbor's house, or picking up the phone and sending our caring thoughts across the wires to a person in need, speaking faithful words to other people often means going to be with them, journeying down the road to the place of meeting, being people of "the Way."

Sister Helen Prejean, a Roman Catholic nun, has a ministry of caring for death row prisoners at the Louisiana State Penitentiary in Angola, and the story of her work was featured in the film *Dead Man Walking.* She uses words, faithful words, to perform her ministry. She

Talking Ourselves into Being Christian

spends much of her life *talking,* speaking to hardened criminals, giving them encouragement and spiritual counsel; she prays with them, she has heard their stories, listened on occasion to their confessions, spoken to them of God's compassion and love; and she has accompanied at least five of them to the place of execution. However, it was not her eloquence, her ability to speak, that first got her involved in this kind of ministry. It was first of all her feet. She felt God calling her to the prison, and as a person of "the Way," she picked up her feet and got moving. "Energy comes to us," she says, "because we get involved in something bigger than ourselves and our hearts have been moved by people's suffering, and we can't remain neutral. We say, 'I don't know what I'm going to do, but I've got to do something. I've got to get involved in some way.'"[7]

Sometimes people wonder how Helen Prejean knows the right words to say. They think about how she talks to murderers, comforts the victims' families, and stands up to the prison officials, and they wonder how she finds the apt and faithful words to speak. In response, she likes to quote a line from Mark Twain's *Huckleberry Finn:* "I went right along, not fixing up any particular plan, just trusting to providence to put the right words in my mouth when the time comes. For I'd noticed that providence always did put the right words in my mouth if I left it alone." As she goes along "the Way," Sister Prejean does the shoe leather part, and God gives her the words to speak.

So to call Christianity "the Way" signals that Christians are people on the move. "The Way" also discloses, and this is the second truth captured in the name, that Christianity is a way of life. The Christian life is a *life,* not just a set of beliefs or ideas but a whole way of living.

Out in the middle of the Chesapeake Bay, not too far as the crow flies from our family's summer place on the Eastern Shore, is Smith Island, Maryland, population 450. Most of people of Smith Island are from old fishing families who have been living off the bay's banquet of crabs, oysters, and rockfish for generations. To be a Smith Islander is not just to be from somewhere; to be a Smith Islander is to live a special kind of way. Because the islanders are beholden to the tides and currents, they watch the weather more attentively and get up in the morning earlier than most of the rest of us to ready the boats for the day's work. Because they live huddled together on a small island, a dot in the bay always at the mercy of the next nor'easter, Smith Islanders attend to each other, care for each other, look out for each other. To be from Smith Island is to eat stewed tomatoes, fresh corn, and crab cakes in the summer; to be worried about the decline in the number of oyster beds; to build one's religious life around meetings and revivals down at the Methodist church; to sing sea songs and shanties that floated over from England and Wales centuries ago; and even to speak in that glorious lilting manner reminiscent of their Elizabethan ancestors. Smith Islanders do everything that other people do. They eat, sleep, work, marry, raise children, sing, dance, bury the dead, and worship God. But they do all of these things according to customs and patterns that, when woven together into a single fabric, mark them off as different. There is no mistaking a Smith Islander. Smith Island isn't just a place; it is a way of life.

In a similar but even deeper sense, Christians have (or should have) a way of life. We are people of "the Way." The Way is not a collection of bizarre religious rituals or unusual customs that set Christians apart from other human beings. In fact, the interesting thing about "the Way," the Christian way of life, is that it is composed of things that all human beings do, but all of them are illuminated and reenvisioned by our relationship to Jesus Christ. For example, all human beings eat—indeed, we have to eat to stay alive. Christians eat too, of course, but Christians attempt to make all meals times of gratitude and thanksgiving; to use a technical term, every meal is a "Eucharist," a fellowship with the risen Christ. Or again, all human beings have children and raise them to be members of society. Christians have and raise children, too, but we raise them, to the best of our ability, to be members of God's society, to be disciples of Jesus Christ. All human communities have to figure out what to do when a stranger shows up: fight or flight or something else? The Christian community, knowing that we were welcomed in Christ when we were strangers to God, tries to show this same kind of hospitality to others.

In other words, the Christian way of life is really just ordinary human life—being born, living together in community, working,

Talking Ourselves into Being Christian

having children, caring for the sick and elderly, eating and drinking, encountering strangers, worshiping, and dying—but all of it refracted through the lens of Jesus Christ, the true human being. Think, for instance, about the very basic human need for a rhythm of restorative rest and meaningful work. All human beings sleep and rise; all human beings have a rhythm of repose and activity, resting and laboring. We all need something to do with our labor that counts, and we all need good rest so that we can get up and do it. Christians are no different. We too rise and wake, rest and labor. Can it be that our relationship to Jesus Christ shapes how we do something so elemental as going to bed and rising to engage the day?

Take the custom of saying a prayer at bedtime. Whether it is a simple "Thank you, O Lord, for this day. Give me rest, give me rest" or the child's prayer, "Now I lay me down to sleep. I pray the Lord my soul to keep" or the ancient night prayer from the sixth century, "Be present, O merciful God, and protect us through the hours of this night, so that we who are wearied by the changes and chances of this life may rest in your eternal changelessness; through Jesus Christ our Lord," by praying at bedside Christians entrust the ending of the day—indeed, all endings—into the hands of a loving God. A woman who battled breast cancer, enduring the chemotherapy, the radiation, and all of the indignities and fears, said, "I have discovered that when I pray at bedtime, I am not just thanking God for this day. I am entrusting all my days and all my nights to God. Evening prayer," she said, "is about living, and it is also practice for dying faithfully, preparing to die not in fear but in trust and hope."

Yes, all people sleep and rise, but Christians can sleep in peace knowing that God rules over all and that we are in God's hands, and Christians can rise knowing that each day is a gift and that by the grace of God, the labor of our hands is not in vain. It makes a difference. It is a part of a whole way of life.

As "the Way," then, Christianity does not desire to be a sect, a narrow little way of being superpious. Instead, Christians want to live together the kind of life they believe God wants all people to live. The Christian community wants to shine like a lamp on a stand and to say to all who will hear, "Look! This is how to be joyfully alive as human beings." As the second-century theologian Irenaeus put it, "The glory of God is humanity fully alive." Christians do not want to set up a sharp division between "us" and "them"—we're Christians and you're not. Rather, Christians want to live in the way that God created all human beings to live, and we believe we can see how to do this by paying attention to the one human being who never failed to live this way: Jesus. To strive to live a fully human life, to live life patterned after Jesus, is the way of Christian faith, and we are "people of the Way." "In the middle of winter," writes Elaine Pagels, "St. Francis called out to an almond tree, 'Speak to me of God!' and the almond tree breaks into bloom. It comes alive. There is no other way of witnessing to God but by aliveness."[8]

So what does this understanding of "the Way" as a total way of life have to do with how Christians talk? What it means is that the goal is to use words as God intends, to learn how to speak in a fully human manner, to learn how to tell the truth, the whole truth, and nothing but the truth. All human beings speak. In fact, one of the things that sets human beings apart from other creatures is that we have the capacity to use complex symbol systems called languages. How do we use language? In many ways—to tell jokes, to cry out in loneliness, to calculate the speed of light, to gossip about a neighbor, to speak of love, to sing joyfully, to curse our bad luck, to call somebody else a hurtful name, to cheat people out of what is rightfully theirs, to establish justice, to comfort someone in distress, to declare war, and to proclaim peace. We have an almost infinite capacity to use words for good or ill, but Christians believe that we are truly human only when we use words like Jesus used them: to bless and not to curse, to build up and not to tear down, to point to the mystery of God pervading all of life and not to refer only, always, and incessantly to ourselves. What we want to do is nothing less than the psalmist's plea, "Let the words of my mouth and the meditations of my heart be acceptable to you, O Lord, my rock and my redeemer" (Psalm 19:14).

At the beginning of this chapter, I said that this book is about how Christians talk about God and faith when we are not in church. What we now know is that heading out into life and talking about God and faith means far more than simply making God noises or

19

engaging in religious talk. We now know that talking about God does not mean sounding like the "Church Lady" on *Saturday Night Live* but instead means talking like strong, loving, and wise human beings. We will talk about God, of course. How could we not? To paraphrase one of the old Christian catechisms, "What does it mean to be human? To glorify God and live joyfully in God forever."[9] We will talk about God, but we will always talk about God in the midst of life—that is, we will be in the midst of life, and God is in the midst of life too. Like Jesus' own parables, so full of farmers and seeds, parents and children, weddings and funerals, baking bread and feasting at table, our faithful talk will be about work and play, parents and children, feasting and fasting, faith and doubt, sickness and health, cruelty and kindness, war and peace, being born and growing old, living and dying.

We need, then, to think of ourselves as more than just "church people," as more than people who go about our daily business and who have a quiet, almost secret compartment in our lives where we are religious. We cannot be human, much less faithful to God, if we keep silent. We must begin to think of ourselves—dare we claim the name?—as *witnesses*.

Chapter 2

CAN I GET A WITNESS?

One morning some years ago, a young bookstore clerk named Deborah arrived at work early to open the shop. Standing at the door waiting for the store to open was a man dressed in the characteristic garments of a Hasidic Jew. As Deborah was unlocking the door, the man quietly asked if he could come in. She hesitated; it was nearly an hour before the store was supposed to open, but the man seemed polite and evidently needed something right away, so she decided to let him come in early. After turning on the lights, she said, "Would you like any help?"

Softly and with an accent he said, "Yes, I want to know about Jesus." This was not an altogether surprising request, since the store specialized in books on religion. So Deborah guided the man upstairs to the shop's ample section of books about Jesus. She pointed to shelves filled with scholarly volumes of Jesus research and books about the early history of Christianity. Then she turned to go back downstairs, but the man called her back.

"No," he said. "I want to know about Jesus the Messiah. Don't show me any more books. You tell me what you believe." Was this man asking for interfaith dialogue? For spiritual counsel? For evangelism? Deborah was unsure. All she knew was that she was being asked what she had almost never been asked before: to put her faith into words.

"My Episcopal soul shivered," she said later, recalling the encounter. "I gulped and told him everything I could think of . . . as much as I could sputter out in my confusion, in the dark."[1]

Deborah's "Episcopal soul shivered," and many of us, regardless of what denominational brand our souls happen to be, would shiver as well. If we were suddenly put in the position of having to express what we believe, many of us would also feel confused and in the dark. Moreover, Deborah recognized that her conversation partner was himself a person of faith, which made visible a truth about all urgent speech: it must be spoken with tenderness and awareness of its impact on others. The man who talked with Deborah eventually chose to be baptized and became a Christian. Deborah was grateful, of course, for his spiritual awakening, but her gratitude was mixed with concern. She did not want what she had said to transgress delicate interfaith boundaries, and she did not want to be any part of any aggressive evangelistic techniques—"winning trophies for God," as she put it. "I am not ashamed of my faith," she wrote. "I am, and will always be, a Christian. But the God I catch glimpses of is a large-hearted God, one to whom all hearts are open. Spiritual arrogance is inexcusable."[2]

A Time to Speak,
A Time to Keep Silence

Being asked to express our faith into words can put us on the spot and causes us discomfort for many reasons, and not all of the reasons are bad ones. We are justified to be quite cautious and even restrained in the use of religious talk. To begin with, many thoughtful Christians recognize that much of what passes for public God talk is often simply the empty God chatter described in Chapter One. It sounds pious, but it's just static on the public airwaves, as hollow as a perfunctory "God bless you" muttered on the subway after a sneeze.

Second, some God talk, though undoubtedly sincere, is downright offensive. Instead of waiting for an invitation to come in, some religious speech puts on hobnail boots and kicks down the door, offending those who hear it and isolating those who use it. I once knew a man, a fundamentalist Christian, who, when greeted with a sociable "Hello, how are you?" would invariably respond, "Saved! How are you?" In the barbershop, at the grocery store, on the street, the reply was the same: a big empty grin and a loud "Saved! How are you?" He no doubt considered this social greeting to be a part of his "witness" and a faithful teaching moment, but the truth is you just wanted to smack him. So people avoided him. Martin Marty, writing in *The Christian Century* about encounters with similarly aggressive God talk, calls this way of talking "in-your-face Christianity," as opposed to "cross-bearing Christianity."[3]

A congressman from the South was once asked why he didn't campaign for gun control, given the fact that polls showed that nearly 70 percent of the voters in his state favored it. "You need to understand the voters in my state," he explained. "Sure, they're in favor of gun control. They just don't like people who go around *talking* about gun control." Likewise, many people who hunger for the experience of God are nevertheless put off by people who go around talking about God all the time, and thoughtful Christians don't want to generate this offense.

Third, and much more deeply, some forms of God talk can actually undermine the very possibility of authentic religious language. The theologian Craig Dykstra, while arguing that religious language is indispensable to faith, also warns that some of the ways church people use this language out in the culture run the risk of falling into self-idolatry. He says:

> When the religious community uses its language simply for self-perpetuation, then God has been captured as the god of the religious cultus and is no longer the God of all of life. And this, in turn, makes the valid use of religious language in everyday life impossible. Insofar as religious language reflects not a pervasive way of life but only the language of an institution or a particular social group within a person's life world, there arises an impermeable wall between religious language as "church talk" and religious language as a foundation for ordinary discourse.

This is the "ghettoization" and ultimate death of religious language.[4]

In other words, sometimes church folk talk about God, but it is actually just a pious form of marketing. We say "worshiping God gives life new meaning" when we are really trying to grow church membership. We say "prayer changes things," but we are really attempting to entice someone to join our prayer group, to reinforce our own religious patterns, and to reassure ourselves that our beliefs are right. We say "society needs to be brought back to godly values," but what we are actually trying to do is to coerce people to vote our way in the next election. Authentic religious language is not about some narrow band of experience called "religion" or "church" or our little view of God's will. It is about everything—the fullness of life, the fullness of being human, the fullness of God's presence in and for the world. Whenever we take the words that describe this fullness and melt them down into something smaller, more manageable, and self-centered, we have gone to the mountaintop but come away with a golden calf. It is idolatry. When we say "God" but we are really just talking about the institution of the church, people quickly sniff out that religious talk is, after all, just advertising, another load of linguistic toxic waste poured into an already polluted stream. The great tragedy is that having heard so much counterfeit God talk, people become numb to the real thing.

Given the dangers, then, why talk about God in public at all? Indeed, many Christians have decided to be doers instead of talkers. They are impressed by the power of what might be called "wordless witness," ways of expressing our faith by actions and character but not with talk. It is quite true, of course, that we proclaim our faith by everything we are and everything we do. Christians witness to the world every day in a thousand silent ways. The tender care of a night nurse, an attorney's rigorous maintenance of integrity, the honesty of an auto mechanic, the truthfulness of a journalist, the patience of a convenience store clerk—all of these forms of service, and many others like them, can be, in their own ways, Christian testimonies.

In one of his celebrated sermons, the theologian Paul Tillich described Elsa Brandström, the daughter of a Swedish diplomat who, as a nurse during World War I, cared for the prisoners in the prisoner of war camps. She fought against the brutality of the guards, against cold, depravation, disease, and hunger. She gave food to the hungry, drink to the thirsty, strength to the sick. When the war was over, she initiated a program to care for the orphans of the war prisoners. "We never had a theological conversation," Tillich said. "It was unnecessary. She made God transparent in every moment. For God, who is love, was abiding in her and she in Him."[5]

So, yes, Christian actions are themselves a form of testimony. Yes, not all religious talk is a good witness and not all good witness involves talk. However, there are times when a silent witness is not enough. There are times when words are called for, when actions alone are not complete and only a word will do. "Always be ready," the writer of 1 Peter says, "to make your defense to anyone who demands from you an accounting of the hope that is within you, yet do it with gentleness and reverence" (1 Peter 3:15). What 1 Peter has in mind are occasions when early Christians needed to come up with words to give meaning to their actions. Specifically, the original readers of 1 Peter were Christians who were being called on the carpet by their neighbors and by the authorities because their actions seemed strange, their customs threatening, and their behavior antisocial. The way Christians endured suffering, turned away from retaliation and violence, honored women, dressed humbly, kept peace in their households, showed hospitality to strangers, and refused to participate in worship of the emperor marked them off as countercultural and made them subject to charges of undermining the stability of society. They were to be prepared for such accusations and ready at any time to explain their faith, gently and reverently. Christians were to be able to say in words how the behavior on the outside was motivated by hope on the inside so that their accusers would at least understand how their faith convictions shaped their way of living.

Such accusations still take place, especially in societies where Christians form a controversial minority group, but for many Christians, like Deborah in the bookstore, the experience of having someone want to know about "the hope that is within you" assumes a gentler, less accusatory form. Our children ask us a question about

God, a topic of importance comes up at the office or the golf course, a neighbor wonders how we view some public issue, a man shows up at the shop asking us to talk about our convictions—a window opens and there is a moment when the right thing to do is to open our mouth and talk about our faith. "Always be ready," 1 Peter urges. Sometimes we are and sometimes we aren't.

In 1986, Susan, a neighbor of mine, found herself with an empty nest and a bit more time to engage some of the interests neglected in the years of raising a family. She decided to get back into the academic swing by taking a spring course at the local community college. Checking the catalogue, she spotted an offering titled "U.S. Foreign Policy: 1945 to the Present." She'd never ventured into politics, and she thought this course might stretch her. It met in the evening, once a week, so it looked convenient, interesting, and challenging. She enrolled. At the first meeting of the course, she was surprised to discover that she and the professor were the only American citizens in the class. The dozen or so other class members were all international students, some of them taking the course as a part of the process of becoming naturalized citizens of the United States.

The course moved along well until mid-April, when newspaper headlines announced that the U.S. military had carried out a bombing raid against Libya, resulting in the deaths of several dozen people. President Reagan said that the air attack was a direct response to the bombing one month earlier of a German nightclub in which American soldiers had been killed and Libyan agents were suspects. Public opinion strongly supported Reagan, viewing the air raids as an appropriate and needed retaliation against Libya and its leaders.

The professor began the next meeting of the class by saying, "We have seen in the news this week a controversial expression of U.S. foreign policy. What reactions do you have?" The students were silent as stones. Finally Susan hesitantly ventured a response. "My husband and I disagree about this," she said, "but I don't think America should have done the bombing."

A young Asian woman in the class looked dumbstruck. "You are the only American I have heard say anything like that," she stammered. "Are you a revolutionary?"

"No," Susan snapped. "I'm a Republican."

"Then why," asked the woman, "why are you against the bombing of Libya?"

Susan said later that she was tempted to respond, "Hey, it's a free country. Everybody's entitled to an opinion," but she sensed that something was at stake here, that something about the situation called for a deeper, more honest response.

"The reason why I disapprove of the bombing," Susan said, "is because of my Christian faith. I know we cannot make foreign policy out of the New Testament, but we are told to 'repay no one evil for evil,' and I just can't rest easy with this." What followed was a spirited and probing conversation, involving the whole class, on balancing love and justice, peace and security, national loyalties and faith commitments, all because the window opened and Susan decided to speak.

GIVING TESTIMONY IN COURT

Given the uncertainties and dangers, as well as the need and urgency, of speaking publicly about faith, it is not surprising that Christians have been thinking for a long time about this matter. As early as the New Testament era, Christians knew that speaking their faith to each other, to their families, and out in the world was difficult, but they also knew that the Christian faith takes shape, grows, and spreads through the spoken word. Learning how to speak the faith, then, was risky but crucial.

From the very beginning, putting the Christian faith into words out in the everyday arenas of life has been called *testimony* or *witness*. These are strong and good words, but they have fallen into corrupt uses, and we need to reclaim them. Often when *witness* and *testimony* are employed in Christian circles, they refer only to autobiographical accounts of how somebody became a Christian. In some settings when a Christian says, "At the meeting the other night I gave my testimony," what she really means is that she told the story of how she developed a deeper relationship with Christ. Taken alone, this use of *testimony* is far too narrow. To be sure, such stories of personal conversion and growth, when they are told truthfully and humbly, are a part of what is meant by testimony, but they are only a fraction the whole meaning.

Witness and *testimony* are big words, and we need to recover their full range of meaning. They are borrowed from the world of the law court, and in a court of law, something important is being contested, something or someone is "on trial." The court is a public place where a decision can be made about this, and in order to make a wise decision, the court needs to know the truth about what happened. So it summons witnesses, people who have seen and heard things pertinent to the trial, and it puts them on the stand to hear their testimony as they tell the truth, the whole truth, and nothing but the truth. Everything depends on the veracity of the witnesses. If they lie or compromise their testimony in any way, the court cannot make a sound judgment. Perjury, bearing false witness, is a serious crime in every society because the ability of a society to hold together ultimately depends on the reliability of the law, which in turn rests on the trustworthiness of testimony.

Christians understand themselves to be in the biggest court case of all, the trial of the ages. What is being contested is the very nature of reality, and everything is at stake. Was the universe created by a loving and just God, or is the universe a blind and random collection of cold stones and burning embers floating through empty space and unshaped by a creative hand? Are human beings created in the image of God and given lives full of purpose and meaning, or is life a "tale told by an idiot, full of sound and fury, signifying nothing"? Are human beings in some deep sense created to be together in communities of trust and harmony, or is the law of the talon and the claw our fate? Is generosity a virtue or a stupidity? Is sacrifice ever noble, or is it just the losing position in a never-ending battle for power? When we stand at the grave of someone we have loved, can we hope to meet again on another shore and in a brighter light, or is this weak sentimentality and a cowardly denial of the brute facts? Everything is before the jury.

Christians believe that we have been summoned to court to tell the truth in this trial. The prophet Isaiah describes how God's people have been subpoenaed as witnesses in a cosmic trial: "You are my witnesses, says the Lord, and my servant whom I have chosen, so that you may know and believe me and understand that I am he. Before me no god was formed, nor shall there be any after me" (Isaiah 43:10). We are not on the witness stand to grow the church, make ourselves look religious, or figure out legal strategy that will ensure that our side "wins." We are witnesses, and we are there for one and only one purpose: to tell the truth about what we have seen and heard. The novelist Reynolds Price once noted that the world is full of stories, but we crave the one, true story we can trust. "While we chatter or listen all our lives in a din of craving—jokes, anecdotes, novels, dreams, films, plays, songs, half the words of our days—we are satisfied only by the one short tale we feel to be true: *History is the will of a just God who knows us.*"[6]

What Price is saying is that Christians are out there in a world full of stories. People are telling stories at the golf club, in the grocery store, on television, and at the PTA meeting: "Did you know the best colleges won't even look at you if you don't make at least 90 percentile on the SAT?" "I got word that Home Depot stock is about to split, and if you want in on the action . . ." "You may have heard that Alice finally had enough and left Bob. He's keeping the children, and . . ." The world is full of stories, but all of these billions of stories are searching for the one, true story, the story of a God who knows and loves us, the story of a God who brings justice to a broken world. Christians are on the witness stand to tell that story, not because it is a likely story or an advantageous piece of testimony, but because it is true. We know it is true because we ourselves have experienced it and witnessed its truth. That is why we are on the witness stand and have taken the oath to tell the truth "so help us God."

Even as we enter the dock, Christians know that we are not the main witness in this trial. The key witness, the witness upon whose testimony the whole trial turns, is none other than Jesus, "the faithful witness" (Revelation 1:5). Everything he said and did was reliable testimony, bearing witness to the God who loves and saves us, to our identity as children of God, and to the hope that can sustain human life. The lower human courts rejected his testimony and, as is sometimes the case with unwelcome testimony, killed the witness (it is no accident that the Greek word for witness is *martyr*). But in a great reversal, on Easter, God validated Jesus' testimony by raising him from the dead. Easter is the announcement that Jesus' witness is true, that his witness cannot be overcome, and that his witness lives even now.

Jesus is the true and faithful witness, and Christians, as a part of God's people, are corroborating witnesses. Our testimony is, in effect, "What Jesus said and did is the truth about God and about human life, and we ourselves can attest in our own lives to the power of this truth."

A friend of mine, Heidi Neumark, served for several years as the pastor of a Lutheran church in the South Bronx, in perhaps the poorest of all poor neighborhoods in America. Her first Sunday as pastor, Heidi understood what kind of church she was serving when she found under the altar a box of rat poison next to the communion wafers. The leaders and officers of her congregation include former addicts and undocumented aliens, the unemployed and the recently homeless. It is the kind of congregation Paul was talking about when he wrote, "Consider your own call, brothers and sisters: not many of you were wise by human standards, not many were powerful, not many of noble birth. But God chose what is foolish in the world to shame the wise" (1 Corinthians 1:26–27).

During Holy Week several years ago, this congregation decided to reenact in a passion play the whole sweep of Holy Week, from Palm Sunday to Easter. They began by dramatizing Jesus' entry into the city, borrowing a live donkey and, led by an actor playing the part of Jesus, parading in a long procession around the block of shabby storefronts and run-down apartments shouting, "Hosanna!" When they got around the block and back to the door of the church, the Palm Sunday procession ran into a street demonstration protesting police brutality. It was fitting, really, as Jesus and the protesters, the congregation and the street crowds, the cries of "Hosanna!" and the cries of social outrage mingled together in a swirl of movement and noise. In fact, someone passing by on the street, seeing the confusion and fearing trouble, even called the police, whose arrival brought a bit of added color and drama. Somehow the processional managed to make it inside the church, where, as the play unfolded, Jesus was tried, condemned, and executed. But then women returned early in the morning of the first day of the week with the amazing word of an empty tomb and the astounding news, "He is risen!" The actors playing the disciples remained true to their assigned parts, expressing disbelief and confidence that this news from the women was but an "idle tale."

But then the script called for three members of the congregation to stand up and give testimony, to bear witness in court as it were, to the truth of the resurrection. "*I know* that he is alive," each one was to begin. The first was Angie. "I know that he is alive," she said, "because he is alive in me." She then told how she was abused by her father, how she fell into despair and alcoholism, became HIV-positive. But then she responded to the welcome of the church, then she started attending worship, then a Bible study, and bit by bit she rose from the grave of her life. Now she is a seminary student, studying to be a pastor. "I am now alive because Jesus Christ lives in me and through me," Angie said, her face aglow. "I am a temple of the Holy Spirit."

The two other witnesses stood in turn, each reciting the assigned part of the script: "I know that he is alive." Then that portion of the play was done, and it was time to move on. But the testimony would not stop. Others in the sanctuary began to rise spontaneously. "I know that he is alive," they would say, "because he is alive in me." Homeless people, addicts now clean, the least and the lost, stood one by one. Nothing could stop them. "I know that he is alive," they shouted, all giving corroborating testimony to the witness of Jesus, adding their own word to the great witness of Easter, telling the truth about what they had seen and heard.[7]

PRACTICE, PRACTICE, PRACTICE

We are not born knowing how to talk about our faith. It is not second nature for us to know how to speak faithfully, how to tell God's story amid all the other stories crowding the landscape of our culture. The ability to give useful and true testimony has to be acquired and learned through experience. Even Jesus, who at age twelve was dazzling the temple leaders with his wisdom had to learn how to speak faithfully. As Luke reminds us, Jesus, like all other faithful people, had to grow in his wisdom and ability (Luke 2:40). How do we learn how to tell the truth about God? It is not just a matter of having experiences, even experiences we would call "religious." One can experience a rainstorm or see a comet blaze across the night sky and still not know what one has experienced. Telling the truth requires experience but also knowledge—a vocabulary and a set of categories to help make sense of things. For Christians, the church is the learning environment for growth in wisdom, the place where the experience of God, which permeates all of life, is given a vocabulary and workable categories. Indeed, one way to think about the church is as the "language school" of God, the place where we learn how to speak faithfully in the whole of our lives.

If you have ever traveled to a another country, perhaps before you went you enrolled in a short language course at the community college or the local Y—"German for Travelers," "Conversational Spanish," "Getting Around in Russian," that sort of thing. Often these courses will toss in a little cultural education. Perhaps on the last night of the course, your teacher wore *lederhosen* to class, served a meal of black bread and borscht, or explained how the locals hail cabs, tip a waiter, or bargain in the street market. The point of such courses is to grasp a bit of the daily language and customs of another culture, to learn how to speak and act in another land. In like manner, in the life of the church, we are in language school learning how to speak and act as people of God, trying to acquire the vocabulary and customs of God's people. We are traveling toward the kingdom of God, and we are trying out phrases, eating the food, and practicing the local customs of that destination. In the church, therefore, we are given words and ways of living that we would never dream of otherwise, not just church words and ways of living, but words and ways of living that shape our pilgrimage every day and in every place.

When children in church school, for example, learn to sing "Jesus loves the little children, all the children of the world. Red and yellow, black and white, they are precious in his sight," they are not merely singing a Sunday School ditty. They are getting ready to speak and act as God's people in a world of many cultures, religions, and races. Or when a congregation every single Sunday of the year sings the psalms, they acquire a vocabulary that touches the raw nerve of every possible human emotion but always come unfailingly around to praise. In doing so, they are worshiping, but they are also in training to know how to speak when out in the world: candidly and honestly, but never cynically or despairingly. "Praise," said C. S. Lewis, "almost seems to be inner health made audible."[8]

On a cold Saturday morning several years ago, I paid a last visit to an old friend. It was the weekend before Christmas, and his neighborhood was gaudy with the usual holiday kitsch: an electric Frosty the Snowman winked from a doorway; a mélange of jolly Santas cavorted across front lawns; a string of reindeer grazed under a cluster of pine trees.

My friend lay in an upstairs bedroom, cared for by loyal friends and tender folks from the hospice, who ushered me to his room and then discreetly left us alone. There was not much to say. This would be his last Christmas, and we both knew it. He could not move from his bed without help, and death, only a few weeks away from claiming him, as it turned out, was already an intruder in the room. Despite the numbing effects of the medicines, he was in constant pain now, his skin an oily gray, his face so taut and ravaged by disease that his expression seemed somewhere between a scream and a smile. We sat mostly silent, a word passing between us now and then, not an awkward silence but more the stillness of old friends content to sit and say farewell with quietness.

Suddenly there was movement downstairs, the sounds of muffled voices, the shuffle of feet. It was a choir from his church come to sing Christmas carols. We could hear them whispering among themselves, trying to decide what to sing. Indeed, what do you sing to a dying man? Their voices started, softly at first, "Lo how a rose e'er blooming . . ." My friend and I looked at each other and waited as the choir slowly climbed the stairs, their voices growing nearer and stronger—"to show God's love aright." The choir was now standing in the doorway. My friend, deep into the darkness of dying and still agonizing hours away from the dawn, turned away so that they would not see his tears as he listened to them as they sang. "She bore for us a savior, when half spent was the night."

The members of this choir had been singing the faith together for a long time, many of them for years. They had spent countless Wednesday nights at rehearsal, mastering the lyrics and the tunes, the meters and the meanings, of hundreds of choral expressions of the faith. They had been trained in the "language school" of the church. As Christians and as human beings, they knew that "the night is dark and we are far from home" and that climbing those stairs toward a dying man while singing something cheery and upbeat like "We wish you a merry Christmas" would be utterly dishonest. They knew they needed to sing both truthfully and hopefully, to lament as well as to rejoice, and so they sang of God's love coming "when half-spent was the night."[9]

Sometimes the wisdom about how to speak as Christians is born of apparent failure. In the 1930s, when the German theologian Dietrich Bonhoeffer was serving as the head of a small seminary in Finkenwald, he proposed a remarkable rule for how the Christians living together in that community, faculty and students alike, ought to talk. As an expression of the gospel, no person in the community, he said, should talk about another Christian in secret, even when the intent is to help and to do good. When Christians speak about each other, Bonhoeffer maintained, they ought to do so truthfully, out in the open, and in the hearing of the person being talked about.

Think about that. If Bonhoeffer's rule were observed among Christians today, there would be no gossip, no secret whispering about others, no strategy meetings on how to handle "difficult" people, no conversations that start "I think we should pray for Randall because . . . ," no coffee hour speculations about whether or not Alice is a "control freak," not even any private sharing about "how best to help Frank and Marilyn" through their marriage problems. Who among us could carry that off? Much of our daily conversation would be silenced.

Hard as they tried, residents of Bonhoeffer's seminary community were not able to abide by the rule either. But by trying, failing, and trying again, the members of that community gained deep insights about the constructive and destructive power of words and were renewed in their commitment to honor other people in everyday speaking. Bonhoeffer's biographer, Eberhard Bethge, observed that by attempting to live by this rule and resolving to try again when they failed, the students and faculty at Finkenwald learned almost as much as they did from sermons and Bible studies.[10]

Whether it is seminary students at Finkenwald going through the day, attending meals and classes and trying to keep Bonhoeffer's rule about speech, or a choir rehearsing next Sunday's anthem at Wednesday night rehearsals and, in the process, learning the power of hopeful lament, these examples, and others like them, point once again to that truth about the Christian faith identified in Chapter One, namely, that Christianity is a way of life, Christians are people of "the Way," and we learn how to be Christian by participating in the life of the Christian community. One cannot go off into the desert on private spiritual retreat and dream up the Christian faith any more than one can become a plumber by dreaming about valves and pipes. One cannot become a Christian by reading a book about Christian doctrine any more than one can become a Texan by reading the works of Larry McMurtry or watching a John Wayne movie. One becomes a plumber by learning from other plumbers how to sweat a joint and rebuild a faucet and then crawling under the sink and getting to work. One becomes a Texan by, well . . . you just have to live there. You have to learn the stories and the lore and master the talk and the walk and the customs and the attitudes. In the same way, one learns how to talk and think and act in Christian ways by living in the midst of the Christian community, becoming tangled up in the messy business of working with, learning with, worshiping with, serving with, talking with, and hanging around with other Christians.

The notion that Christianity is a way of life learned in the midst of others seems, at first glance, to be obvious, but it runs against the grain of how religion is often understood in our culture. In the popular mind,

Christians are people who believe certain things, and Jews and Muslims and Buddhists are people who believe certain other things. In other words, religion is defined exclusively as a set of beliefs held to be true by individuals. This is why the door-to-door pollsters always find more religious people out there in apartments and homes than ever show up in synagogues, churches, mosques, and other houses of worship. (Given the facts that most people in North America profess belief in God and yet a far more modest number regularly attend worship, someone once quipped that the Gallup poll ought to ask people, "What religion are you currently not practicing?")

So what does it mean to be a Christian? Some would say that a Christian is a person who belongs to a church. A Presbyterian, a Catholic, a Methodist. Some would go deeper and say that a Christian is one who believes certain things. God was in Christ, the tomb was empty, Jesus is Lord. But as we have been claiming, belonging and believing, important as they are, are not the only ways to describe a Christian. A Christian is a person who pursues a certain way of life. This way of life involves beliefs, and it is done together with others, but the beliefs and the belonging are gathered up and expressed in the ways that Christians live life.

My stepson was a star cross-country runner in high school. He belonged to the cross-country team with the same zeal a devout Episcopalian might feel toward the local parish. What is more, his cross-country involvement entailed a whole set of beliefs—doctrines really—about nutrition, exercise, and aerobics. He believed, for example, that fueling up on carbohydrates the night before a race gives extra energy and that cool-down periods after a meet are important to avoid injury. But belonging to the team and having certain convictions did not make him a runner. It was the disciplines of running. Along with the others on the team, he pursued an extraordinary way of life. He met other runners many mornings at dawn to run several miles. He ate a special diet, refused to drink sugary sodas, and went to bed early before meets. He learned this way of life from his coach and from his older teammates, and he made it his own. The team picture in the high school yearbook merely shows that he was on the team. Getting up at 5:30 A.M. to run seven miles with his teammates is what made him a runner.

Similarly, Christianity is a way of life, a set of practices. These practices grow out of and embody our beliefs, and they are done with other Christians. Talking about God, giving testimony, is one of these practices. Talking about God involves much more than simply opening our mouths and saying whatever comes to mind about our religion. Down through the centuries, Christians have learned a thing or two about how to speak, when to speak, what words to use, and how to listen to others as well.

A recent television commercial depicts a monastery where the monks, though dedicated to silence, nonetheless use their computers to send each other silent instant messages about worldly matters, such as the baseball scores ("Padres win!"). It is a witty commercial, but actually not too far from the truth. Christian communities have always experimented with the forms of communication—what to say and how to say it—that are best suited to express the gospel mission. In the early monastic movement, for example, communities of monks dedicated themselves to a life of contemplation and prayer. Some of these monastic communities had a rule that "when a monk speaks, he must do so gently and without laughter, humbly, gravely, with few and reasonable words, and that he be not boisterous in his speech, as it is written: A wise man is known by the fewness of his words."[11] This does not mean that a Christian must never laugh or that Christian speech must always be grave. What it means is that in the monastery, given the setting and the vocation of the monks, humble and quiet speech did the best job of conveying the gospel. It's like fueling up on carbs before a cross-country race. It's part of the discipline, part of the practice.

But where and how do we learn this practice in our own setting? Most of us aren't in monasteries, so how do we learn how talk about God at work, at the grocery store, at the swimming pool, over the backyard fence? Fortunately, we do not have to do this by ourselves, and we do not have to become virtuosos of religious speech. Learning how to speak faithful words is something that we learn together in the church. Christians have been trying to talk faithfully for two millennia, and we have discovered a few things along the way that can be passed along. Not only that, Christians have a language school, an academy where we can acquire the vocabulary and grammar of faithful speech and where we can practice what to say and how to say it. This language school is Christian worship, and it is there that we must go next.

Chapter 3

SUNDAY WORDS

Several years ago, the legendary Appalachian folk singer Ralph Stanley issued a two-volume recording of bluegrass and mountain songs. Tellingly, the first volume was called *Saturday Night,* and the second was titled *Sunday Morning.* The separation between the two was wide. *Sunday Morning* was about "preachin', prayin', and singin'," while *Saturday Night* was about the "real stuff" of life, like working hard, raising children, seeking joy, having your heart broken, trying to stay sober, taking care of Mama and Daddy, dealing with betrayal, finding one's way down the highway of life, and facing death. Worship, church, and Sunday were on one side of the ledger, and the Saturday stuff of life was on the other.

Unfortunately, many of us have this same split playing in our heads all the time. There is the "Sunday morning" experience of prayers, hymns, sermons, and there is the "Saturday night" (and we can add the "Monday afternoon") experience of kicking up our heels, balancing the checkbook, building a career, deciding who we are, dealing with relationships, and generally figuring out how to find some purpose and joy in the things we do and say every day.[1] On the one side is the religious side of us, and on the other is the "just trying to be human and make it through life" side. We go to worship, and we sing the hymns, pray the prayers, listen to the sermons, and then we go back out into the real world, where we have to deal with the mundane realities of life and make compromises and hard choices.

Much of our ability to put faith into words outside of church depends, however, on seeing the connections between "Sunday morning" and "Saturday night," between the words we use in worship and the words we speak the rest of the week. This does not imply, of course, that Christian witness necessarily means going around quoting sermons at dinner parties, whistling hymns at Little League games, or reading Paul's epistles at business conferences. Nor does it mean that we go in the other direction, stripping our Sunday services of the special language of worship in a desperate attempt to sound more like "Saturday night" and thus to be more relevant. The connections between Sunday worship and the workaday week are far more subtle and complex than that. What we need is to discover how the dinner party, the Little League game, the business meeting, and all other aspects of our Monday-to-Saturday world are already present in worship, woven into the very fabric of prayer, hymn, and sermon.

Likewise, the central truth of Sunday worship, the living and active presence of God, is also true at the dinner party, the Little League game, and the business meeting. God's favorite time of the week is not necessarily Sunday morning. God does not love only the church and does not live only in sanctuaries. God loves the whole world, and Christ is alive in the whole world, which means that the world, for all its terror and pain, is also a place of wonder, grace, and holy presence. Tuesday afternoon is as full of the Spirit as is Sunday morning. Good worship transforms how we live our everyday lives, but how we live, work, eat, rest, sing, dance, spend, relate to others, hope, grieve, fight, and laugh also affects our worship. Worship informs and changes life, and life informs and changes worship; perceiving the reciprocity between "Sunday morning" and "Saturday night" enables us both to worship as people who have real lives in the world and to live as people who are in worshipful relationship to God.

MAKING THE CONNECTIONS

Most Christians know, of course, that this split between Sunday morning and the rest of life is a false separation. We know that there is supposed to be an organic and vital connection between our Sunday worship and who we are and the way we live the rest of the week, but how should we describe that connection? Christians will often say things like "Worship helps me get through the week. I couldn't make it Monday to Saturday without worshiping on Sunday" or "Worship is where I get my spiritual batteries charged." There is truth in this, of course. Worship at its best can be truly uplifting and inspiring, and worship can fortify us for the mundane tasks of life. But it is finally too shallow to think of worship mainly as a kind of holy pep rally aimed at giving us the spiritual energy to get out there in the workaday world and shoulder life's burdens.

Worship does more than inspire us; it transforms us. It changes the way we live, changes the way we view life's challenges, changes what truly matters to us, changes the way we see ourselves and others. If worship is only a way to get pumped up so that we can "keep on keeping on," then worship can too easily be reduced to a means to perpetuate the way we are already living. But worship is about more than spiritual motivation. It is about vision and hearing, and worship gives us new eyes and ears, a new set of lenses to look at the world, a new vocabulary allowing us to listen afresh and speak what we could not have said before. To see and hear differently is to live differently, to have the ways we think and feel, make decisions and act as Christians transformed.

How, then, can we make better sense of the connection between Sunday worship and the rest of life? First, we can shift the way we tend to think sequentially about the relationship of Sunday to the rest of the week. First, we say, there is Sunday (that's the day for worship), then comes Monday (that's the day we start the workweek), and so on, as if the days of the week were like eggs in a carton, all in a row and each with its separate compartment. But the relationship between Sunday, as a day of worship, and the rest of the week is not just one of sequence, it is a matter of *depth*. Sunday is not just one more day in a string of days. Rather, Sunday, as the day of worship, is the essence of the week, the Day of all Days, the day that discloses what is deep and hidden, but nonetheless true, about every day. Sunday worship is like the key scene in a play where suddenly everything in the rest of the drama becomes clear and all the characters are seen in a true light. Or again, just as a rainbow displays the colors that are always present, but not apparent, in ordinary daylight, so Sunday worship refracts and makes visible what is true every day, that God is Lord over all days, over all time.

The physicist Neils Bohr, the father of quantum mechanics, once said that the first inkling he had about the nature of the universe came when he was a child gazing into the fish pond at his family home. For hours on end, he would lie beside the pond, watching the fish swimming in the water. One day he realized with a start that the fish he was watching did not know that they were being watched. The fish were unaware of any reality outside the pond. Sunlight streaming in from the outside was, to the fish, simply an inner illumination contained within the pond. Even when it rained, the fish saw this not as an event from the outside but only as ripples and splashes enclosed in their environment. Bohr wondered if humans were like the fish in this regard, being acted on in multiple dimensions of reality but aware of only our limited frame of reference.

What if Sunday worship were the chance to lie down beside life's pond and to realize that what often looks and sounds on any given Monday like events contained within the pond are actually interventions from another realm? What if Sunday allowed us to get up on Monday morning and to see and hear what is hidden from Monday-only eyes and ears, that God is present and at work in every corner of life? Then we wouldn't talk about "Sunday morning" and "Saturday night" as two separate realms. Rather we would know that Sunday morning shows us what is really happening, what is really true, about Saturday night. We also would not so easily say things like "We go to church to worship on Sunday, and then we go back out into the 'real world.'" As theologian and pastor William H. Willimon has noted, this expression has it backward. Worship is the "real world"; at its most profound, worship is a way of "entering the world as it really looked in its full, transparent reality," a place where we hear and see and experience what is genuinely true, unmasking the illusions of the world outside.[2]

This leads to the second way we can make a connection between Sunday worship and the rest of life. This is perhaps an unusual way to put it, but we can recognize that worship forms a kind of dress rehearsal for the drama of the Monday-to-Saturday world. The actions and patterns of worship—the prayers, hymns, sermons—are not just the ceremonies of worship. They anticipate and shape what we say and do in the rest of life.

In *Open Secrets,* Richard Lischer's memoir about his first pastorate at Cana Lutheran Church, a small congregation in rural Illinois, he has a delightful description of how Sunday worship rehearses the words we say and the deeds we do in the workaday world. "In Cana," he writes, "we baptized our babies, celebrated marriages, wept over the dead, and received Holy Communion—all by the light of our best window." What Lischer calls "our best window" was an intricate and brilliantly colored stained-glass window that the congregation had ordered out of a catalogue from a studio in Chicago and installed high above the altar. Even though it was beautiful, the window had a most serious purpose, boldly depicting, in glass and light, nothing less than the doctrine of the Trinity. In the center of the window was a triangle enclosing the word *Deus,* Latin for "God," and around this triangle were the words *Pater, Filius,* and *Spiritus Sanctus*—Father, Son, and Holy Spirit. Lines in the window—"little highways," Lischer calls them—depicted the connections and interrelationships among these persons of the Godhead. The little flock at Cana Lutheran worshiped every Sunday with the paths of God's own life shining down on them, and as they did, Lischer says, they began to understand that the paths of their Monday-to-Saturday lives could be reflections of this divine pattern:

> We believed there was a correspondence between the God who was diagramed in that window and our stories of friendship and neighborliness. . . . An aerial photographer once remarked that from the air you can see paths, like canals on Mars, that crisscross pastures and fields among the farms where neighbors have trudged for generations, just to visit or help one another in times of need. These, too, are the highways among *Pater, Filius,* and *Spiritus Sanctus* grooved into human relationships. The word *religion* comes from the same roots as *ligaments.* These are the ties that bind.[3]

A Test Case: The Gathering

The connections between worship and the rest of our lives are not something we have to force or to make happen. They are already in place, and it is a matter of our being able to see them and to realize their importance. To get a taste of how worship and life interpenetrate, let us consider a seemingly routine moment in worship: the gathering. Congregations differ on how they do this, but simply put, the gathering, as the first act in a service of worship, involves all the people who will worship—clergy and congregation—coming into the place of worship. Sometimes this is quite informal, even random. People just arrive at the church and either go to their usual pews or are guided by ushers to available spots. In other congregations, people convene around a coffeepot in the fellowship area, noisily catching up on each other's lives, until the bell rings for worship and they move into the worship space. In still other settings, the gathering takes the form of choir and clergy processing solemnly down the center aisle to their places in the chancel. Sometimes the worship leader will signal the start of worship by calling out a cheerful "Good morning!" or "Grace and peace to you in the name of Jesus Christ!" Sometimes there will be a presentation of announcements, joys, and concerns. Regardless of the details of how it is done, though, the gathering involves the people coming from their distinct places to be together for worship. People move from their separate lives to the place of corporate worship, from being not-a-congregation into being a congregation.

Now if we think about it, a gathered congregation is an odd thing. Almost every congregation includes an unusual mix of people. While it is true that many Christians worship in neighborhood churches or choose to worship in congregations of people who are broadly similar in background, it is also true that almost every congregation has a measure of diversity. To put this bluntly, look around you the next time you are in worship, and you will almost surely see at least several people you would not choose to be with in any other setting. Be assured, also, that others could look in your direction and say the same thing. Congregations are not just clubs or social cliques; they are to some degree microcosms of God's society, small mirrors of the diverse humanity whom God's calls together. Even when congregations fight and split and get down to a handful of folks "just like us," God has a way of sending a stranger, a visitor, and the diversity begins all over again.

So there we are, gathered for worship. There is the veterinarian who takes care of my pet. There is the kid who works behind the counter at Blockbuster Video, the man who runs the cash register at Wal-Mart, the woman who serves as principal of the local middle school, and the couple who ride the van in from the retirement center. Suddenly we are not just individual folks but a gathering of God's people, and I am in relationship with all of these people. Outside of worship, I barely know some of these people; some I know not at all. Some of these people I do know outside of worship, but perhaps not all the relationships are good and sweet. There is the plumber who left a job half-finished at my house, the legislator I voted against in the last election, the tenth-grade history teacher who gave my son a failing grade. We are an odd bunch in here, real life and ambiguities jostling shoulder to shoulder in worship.

But in worship I am invited to look at this gathering of people with new eyes. I am reminded in worship that I did not gather these people; God did. It wasn't my idea to pull together such an unlikely lot; it was God's idea, and I am summoned to see everyone present as a brother or sister in faith. As if that were not enough of a stretch, I am even invited in my faithful imagination to see this gaggle of teachers and merchants and farmers and dentists as the very beloved of God, created in the image of God, a royal priesthood, citizens of a holy nation, without forgetting for a minute that they are, at one and the same time, quite ordinary folks with all the real-life struggles and problems any collection of human beings possesses.

Worship trains us to have this sort of double vision about other people, to see people, including ourselves, as flawed and broken but also as created, chosen, and beloved by God. Such vision takes practice, and that is why we worship every week. We cannot get this sort of vision, cannot maintain this sort of vision, through a onetime mountaintop experience. It takes training, repetition, and practice. So every week we come to worship and have the gathering moment.

What difference does this make? It has been said that if we really knew how to see with the eyes of our souls, we would see angels going before every person we meet, saying, "Make way for the image of God! Make way for the image of God!" As simple as the gathering for worship is, it shapes in us a vision of other people as the royalty of God. Once we have been trained in worship to see people as the treasures of God, we can't look at the kid in Blockbuster Video or the cashier at Wal-Mart the same way anymore. These people are God's very own children, even if they do not know it yet. We become alert to the ways and places in life where people are treated as if they were just numbers or just consumers or just problems or just trash rather than the miracles they truly are.

Thomas Merton, who became famous for his devotional writing, was a Trappist monk who spent much of his adult life in worship at a Kentucky monastery. One day, however, he happened to be in downtown Louisville, and suddenly the rhythms of worship began to reverberate in the life of the street. He writes:

> In Louisville, on the corner of Fourth and Walnut in the center of the shopping district, I was suddenly overwhelmed with the realization that I loved all these people, that they were mine and I was theirs, that we could not be alien to one another, even though we were total strangers. I have the immense joy of being human, a member of the race in which God himself became incarnate. As if the sorrows and stupidities of the human condition could overwhelm, now that I realize who we really are. If only everybody could understand this! But it cannot be explained. There is no way of convincing people that they are walking around shining like the sun.[4]

Because worship enabled him to see people in a new way, Merton has a visionary experience on the streets of Louisville. But it works in the other direction as well. To see the full range of humanity out there in the world "shining like the sun" makes us wonder why our churches are sometimes so narrow, sometimes to inhospitable, sometimes so governed by the same barriers that exist between people in society. In other words, worship gives a vision of a fuller and richer way of life in the world, and that vision conversely pushes us toward a richer, more faithful, and more just form of worship.

GOD'S SOUNDTRACK

What is true about every aspect of worship is true about speech as well. The way we talk in worship affects the way we talk in the rest of our lives, and vice versa. In the place of worship, we cannot pray or sing faithfully without our words being full of the sorrows and joys of life. Conversely, the words of worship—prayer words, sermon words, hymn words, Bible words, creedal words, words of praise and penitence, protest and pardon—are like stones thrown into the pond; they ripple outward in countless concentric circles, finding ever fresh expression in new places in our lives.

Worship is, as I have said, a key element in the church's "language school" for life. The point is not to go through life speaking in a "stained-glass voice." The point is to let the language of worship shape our witness outside of the sanctuary. If, for example, a corporation trustee feels compelled to speak out against a management plan to strip-mine Montana, he may not quote the psalm he heard in church last Sunday—"The earth is the Lord's and the fullness thereof"—but those words spoken in worship may well guide him toward what he will say, may well subtly shape how he communicates concern about stewardship of the creation and the care of the earth.

A friend of mine wrote recently about the rather mundane but vexing experience of driving through the clogged city streets to get to work on Monday morning. To ease the journey, he popped in a cassette tape of music he had purchased when his family, on vacation in Scotland, had toured Saint Giles Cathedral in Edinburgh. The rich sound of the Saint Giles choir singing a Good Friday hymn, Bach's arrangement of "O Sacred Head Now Wounded," began to fill his car as he negotiated his way through the traffic. The words of that great hymn blended in with the honking horns and the hum of morning traffic: "What Thou, my Lord, hast suffered was all for sinners' gain:

Mine, mine was the transgression, but Thine the deadly pain. Lo, here I fall, my Savior! 'Tis I deserve Thy place."

Suddenly, this hymn, so familiar from worship but now being heard in a different place—in a car, in rush hour traffic—started to heighten the man's awareness of the world around him. "Idling in rush hour traffic . . . ," he wrote, "the woman in the Infiniti next to me adjusted her rear-view mirror for the morning ritual of lipstick. The soundtrack punched through into my consciousness: ''Tis I deserve Thy place.' And yet Jesus died not just for me but also for her! Somehow, it made her far less easy for me to dismiss there in the traffic." The words of the hymn cast a different light on others along the journey as well. A family in a car with two children bouncing up and down in the backseat, a nearly toothless woman on the sidewalk with a backpack and brightly colored socks, a jogger, a young mom with a baby in a three-wheeled carriage. "'Tis I deserve Thy place," the choir sang, prompting the man to say to himself, "Jesus died not just for me," the man thought, "but for them too!"

When he got to work that day, he reflected on the experience of the commute, the intersection of the hymn and the sights of the world around him. "Embracing the faith is a little like having a special soundtrack," he wrote. "It's a little like hearing, as if for the first time, an often distant, not always immediately perceptible, song being sung beneath all other experiences. And when we're tuned to that song, it makes a difference. It gives us the ability to see the world and those who dwell therein as God sees it all."[5]

It's a provocative idea—worship as a soundtrack for the rest of life, the words and music and actions of worship inside the sanctuary playing in the background as we live our lives outside, in the world. It happens all the time. The preacher says somewhere in the Sunday sermon that "God's grace is present in the broken places of life," and the words come back to challenge and comfort when the telephone rings late at night with sad news. "I believe in the forgiveness of sins," cries the old creed, and the phrase lingers in our mind when we discover that a colleague at work has not been altogether trustworthy. On Sunday we pray, "Almighty God, unto whom all hearts are open, all desires known, and from whom no secrets are hid," and on Thursday night, when we are by ourselves in the house and the day has been hard and we are feeling alone and misunderstood, the words of the prayer come back to reassure us that we are indeed known, known to our depths by God. The conversation at the office coffeepot turns to politics, and someone says that he's tired of paying hard-earned tax dollars to feed other people's kids. Suddenly we remember a line from last Sunday's Scripture lesson, "Bear one another's burdens, and in this way you will fulfill the law of Christ," and we know we are compelled to respond with a different word.

GOING TO WORSHIP AND LEARNING TO TALK

Something of the relationship between the words of worship and everyday speech can be seen in Psalm 19. When biblical scholars study this psalm, most of them find it to be a patchwork quilt at best and a confusing tangle at worst. It begins with a hymn about God in nature ("the heavens are telling the glory of God"), then shifts abruptly to a wisdom psalm about Scripture ("the law of the Lord is perfect"), and shifts once more to a completely different type of psalm, one of personal devotion ("let the words of my mouth and the meditation of my heart be acceptable to you, O Lord"). The three sections of the psalm have different poetic structures, employ different vocabularies, and seem to come from widely diverging historical periods. The psalm is like a rambling old house with several additions, each done by a different owner and in a different style.

When we stand back, though, and look at Psalm 19 in its entirety, we can glimpse a unity in what first seems to be disjointed fragments. Taken as a whole, this is a psalm about speech, about words.[6] It begins with the psalmist listening to nature talking about God:

> The heavens are telling the glory of God;
> and the firmament proclaims his handiwork.
> Day to day pours forth speech,
> and night to night declares knowledge. (vv. 1–2)

In other words, the psalmist is out there in nature, perhaps lying on a hill gazing up at the sky. As the sun rolls across the heavens, turning from pale yellow to orange to red, the psalmist can hear the whole creation singing a hymn and preaching a sermon. But then something strange happens:

> There is no speech, nor are there words;
> their voice is not heard. (v. 3)

This odd verse, difficult to translate from Hebrew, is a startling interruption of the heavenly speech. For whatever reason, the psalmist admits that he cannot hear what is being said, cannot make out the words. There is a hymn being sung by the universe, but the psalmist cannot make out the lyrics. So he goes to worship:

> The law of the Lord is perfect,
> reviving the soul;
> the decrees of the Lord are sure,
> making wise the simple.
> The precepts of the Lord are right,
> rejoicing the heart;
> the commandment of the Lord is clear,
> enlightening the eyes. (vv. 7–8)

The psalmist has now gone into the sanctuary, into the place of worship, where he hears the reading of Scripture and the story of God. The speech of worship clarifies the holy speech out in the world, and only when his hearing is tuned by the speech of worship can the psalmist fully hear the hymn of praise being sung in nature.

The psalmist has traveled from nature into worship, from the speech of the heavens to the speech of temple, but there is yet one more move to make. The psalmist himself will now open his mouth and join in with the praise of God:

> Let the words of my mouth
> and the meditations of my heart

be acceptable to you,
O Lord, my rock and my redeemer. (v. 14)

The psalmist has now become a witness, testifying in worship and in the rest of life to the presence and praiseworthiness of God. He prays that his words will be "acceptable," that he will tell the truth, the whole truth, and nothing but the truth.

This is not to say, though, that even the words of worship are always good and true.

BLAH, BLAH, BLAH

A seminary student, just learning how to preach, was once invited to speak at a vesper service at a local nursing home. The service was held in the lobby of the home, and many of the residents, some in wheelchairs, made their way from their rooms assisted by nurses and aides. One of the gifts of great age is the freedom to speak one's mind freely and openly, and during the opening part of the service, which involved the singing of several favorite hymns, a number of residents blurted out extemporaneous comments. When it was time for the sermon, though, the room grew quiet. The student had spoken only a few sentences, however, when a stooped woman seated on an electric scooter suddenly whirred the scooter around and headed back to her room shouting, "Blah, blah, blah!"

It was a disconcerting moment for the student, to say the least, but understanding the situation, she managed to recover. Truthfully, though, most of us have had moments in worship when, if we were being forthright, we too would have muttered, "Blah, blah, blah." I have been trying to make the case that the words of worship can shape our witness in the rest of life, but we need to be honest and admit that not all worship words are good words. We have all experienced worship that is flat, banal, and boring. Human beings have the freedom to craft worship, and we do not always craft well. Hence worship sometimes involves the wrong words, words that miss the mark, words that never take flight, words that suffer from being overworked, or even words that are downright deceptive. Thomas Merton once complained that the marvelous affirmation "God is love" has been used so often and so thoughtlessly that to say it in our day is like saying "Eat Wheaties."

The words of worship can sometimes be empty, trivial, hurtful, artless, irrelevant, pompous—or just plain too numerous. The author Kathleen Norris, after attending Sunday worship for several weeks at a certain church, complained that "what struck me most forcibly . . . was the sheer quantity of verbiage. It felt like a word bombardment, and I often needed a three-hour nap to recover." Norris began to wonder "why people in a religion of the Word were so often careless with their words used in worship."[7]

Indeed, church worship services can seem infected by the same glut of words that plagues us in the rest of life. From the morning newspaper to the television talk show to e-mail and voice mail to conversation over lunch to the billboards on the highway to political speeches to the telephone sales pitch to bumper stickers, we are inundated with words, in some ways besieged by talk, much of it empty and cheap. We are assailed by so many words that like an inflated currency, words tend to lose their value and persuasive power. As Eliza Doolittle said to her suitors in *My Fair Lady,* "Words, Words, Words! . . . Is that all you blighters can do? Don't talk of stars shining above; if you are in love—*show* me!"[8]

THE TALKING GOD

Given the perils of wordiness and clichés in worship, we may be tempted to wish for worship liberated from language altogether. Silent reflection, for example, or a wordless dance of praise or a simple embrace of reconciliation—acts of worship that float lightly through air, completely free of the weight of words, often seem preferable to a barrage of words. Indeed, some Christians seek to soar above the mundane words of everyday speech to the ecstatic sounds of glossolalia, "speaking in tongues" or to a wordless sense of union with God.

Nevertheless, worship eventually comes around to words. Silence in Christian worship is always expectant silence, awaiting the next word or reflecting on the previous one. Action in worship is always significant action, which implies that somewhere a word has been spoken to provide meaning, and ever since the Apostle Paul wrote to the Corinthians about speaking in tongues, no ecstatic speech in worship has been complete without an interpretation, and "one who speaks in a tongue should pray for the power to interpret" (1 Corinthians 14:13). Christian worship inevitably takes shape in words.

In fact, this bond between worship and words is no accident; it is built into the very essence of the gospel and of our relationship to God. Christians think of worship as a vast conversation with God, a dialogue between humans and the divine that is often structured but sometimes free-flowing and spontaneous, sometimes intimate and sometimes formal, sometimes harmonious and other times confrontational, on occasion quite personal and at other times communal. Sermons are not just thoughts for the day; at their deepest and best, they are understood to be God speaking to human beings. Hymns are not just songs to enliven the time and enhance the mood; they are most often prayers and vows, declarations of faith and promises, expressions of praise and thanksgiving—in short, words spoken to God, words spoken about God, and words spoken in response to God. When Kathleen Norris complains about too many words and careless words in worship, it reflects her hunger—and ours, perhaps—for beautiful words, true words, healing words, thoughtful words, saving words.

Indeed, Christians experience God as one who speaks and who invites speech in return. In the main, Christians do not have an abstract, philosophical concept of God; rather, they understand God primarily through the stories in the Bible, and according to these stories, God is quite a talker. Hardly three verses into Genesis, God already breaks the silence. "Let there be light," God says, and nothing has been the same since. God speaks, and the universe comes into being. God speaks, and human life changes. God says things like "Go from your country and your kindred and your father's house to the land I will show you" or "Comfort, O comfort my people" or "Whom shall

53

I send?" When God speaks, people respond—"Here am I, send me!" or "Woe is me!"—and when God is silent, people cry out, "O God, do not keep silence." Even Jesus is understood to be a message from God, an expression of God's speech: "Long ago, God spoke to our ancestors in many and various ways by the prophets, but in these last days he has spoken to us by a Son" (Hebrews 1:1).

This is a metaphor, of course, this idea of God speaking. To say that God speaks is a symbolic way of describing the totality of God's interaction with us and with creation, but worship embodies and represents this interaction by arranging an exchange of word, thus enabling a conversation between God and humanity. The call to worship is announced—"Praise the Lord! Sing to the Lord a new song!"—and what is this but a shout from across the river from a God who wishes to engage us in holy conversation, a word from beyond intruding into the chatter of everyday speech and summoning a new and urgent dialogue? "Holy, Holy, Holy," sings the congregation, and what is this but an awestruck response to this disruption? "We have wandered from your ways like lost sheep," the people pray, and what is this but an honest outpouring to God of all human guilt and shame, truthful admission of the shadows that fall across our lives? "Go in peace; your sins are forgiven," intones the worship leader, but what is this but a response from God to our penitence? Back and forth the words of worship flow, moving like the shuttle of a loom, steadily weaving the subtle patterns of the relationship between God and humanity.

Christian worship is not only a dialogue, a dramatic conversation, between God and humanity; it is also, as I have been claiming, a kind of dress rehearsal for human speech outside of the sanctuary. To worship is not only to hear and speak truthful and life-changing words inside the sanctuary but also to prepare ourselves for truthful and life-changing speech in the other areas of life. This is why I have called worship God's language school, a place where we are trained to speak in new ways and given the vocabulary to express a new reality.

The words of worship can enable ordinary speech out in life to become, in its own way, holy speech. The kind of genuine, emotionally rich, hopeful, faithful, courageous, grittily honest speech that makes up truthful worship is countercultural in a world where talk is often cheap and evasive, and it prepares us for speaking in the rest of our lives in ways that are surprisingly fresh and hopeful and healing. As Craig Dykstra puts it in his book *Growing in Faith,* "Religious faith is a way of living that intends to be in touch with what is true and real. But it implies that to see, understand, and live rightly requires living in a particular way. This means that religious language is not just language about 'religious things' (i.e., the religious community, its institutions, and traditions), but is about the whole of reality made evident and available through the community's faith."[9] In a world where talk is cheap, where we are pummeled all day long by words, words, words, there is a deep hunger for the right word, the true word, the word of grace and hope. Like a monarch butterfly in a field full of gray moths, an honest word, a loving word, a faithful word sings and soars and stands out by its very contrast.

In his book *The Culture of Disbelief,* Stephen Carter describes how, when he speaks to civic groups, he often addresses the topic "The Most Dangerous Children in America." To introduce this theme, Carter tells two stories. The first is about the terrifying day that his daughter, five years old at the time, was caught in the crossfire of a gun battle between rival gangs in Queens. Adding to the terror was the fact that Carter and his daughter were separated by the gunfire, and he could not get to her until the shooting stopped. When Carter tells this story, his audience generally gasps in horror and sympathy.

Then Carter relates another personal experience. He was commuting on the train from his home in Stamford, Connecticut, to New Haven. As the train made its various stops, many teenagers got on board, headed for private schools along the train's route. At one stop, a group of girls got on, and Carter happened to overhear their conversation. They were heatedly debating which community was the most fashionable and exclusive, Westport or Fairfield. One of the girls, from Westport, named a person of great wealth who lived in her town, only to be countered by a Fairfield girl, who named an even wealthier resident of her community.

The argument raged back and forth until one of the Westport girls came up with an announcement she clearly saw as a trump card.

She named a world-famous entertainer who, she claimed, actually lived in Westport. Not true, said one of the Fairfield girls. The entertainer did not live in Westport but was only visiting a friend there. She knew this for a fact, she said, because she had met this entertainer at her father's store.

Hearing this, the Westport girl raised up and hooted disdainfully, "Your father has a *store*?" The Fairfield girl, realizing too late that she had said too much, cringed in shame as the Westport girl drove the blade home. "What does he sell there?" she crowed. "*Hardware?*"

After telling these two stories, Carter asks his audience which of the two groups of children is the more dangerous, the Queens gang members or the private school girls. Predictably, most of Carter's hearers will say that the gang members are the more dangerous. But then Carter points out that the gang members, violent as they are, are closed in by their neighborhood, and most of them will likely be dead or in jail before long. The girls on the train, though, are attending the best schools in the land. They will no doubt be admitted to the finest universities and will go on to important careers where they will make decisions that will affect many other people. In the long run, the words they speak and the attitudes behind them may in fact be more lethal than the gang's bullets.[10]

Carter heard these children—our children—using language in a way that is all too familiar in our society: language used to hurt, to demean, to devalue human beings, to embody questionable values or class and wealth.

Is there another language available, a language that counters this destructive use of words? In her story "Temple of the Holy Ghost," Flannery O'Connor tells of other school-aged girls, two fourteen-year-olds, who provoke themselves to convulsive laughter by calling each other "Temple One" and "Temple Two." They are making fun of Sister Perpetua, the oldest nun at their school, who told their class what to do if a young man should "behave in an ungentlemanly manner with them in the back of an automobile." They were to say: "Stop sir! I am a Temple of the Holy Ghost!"

As the story goes, these two girls are invited for the weekend to the home of a woman and her twelve-year-old daughter. Caught in another episode of the giggles, the girls gleefully tell their host about Sister Perpetua and what she said. To their surprise, the woman does not join their laughter but in a serious voice tells them, "I think you girls are pretty silly. After all, that's what you are—Temples of the Holy Ghost." The girls are more astonished than impressed, suddenly wary that their host "was made of the same stuff as Sister Perpetua." However, the exchange is overheard by the host's twelve-year-old daughter, who takes it all in and marvels at the idea: "I am a Temple of the Holy Ghost, she said to herself, and was pleased with the phrase. It made her feel as if somebody had given her a present."[11]

Here a phrase borrowed from worship—"Temple of the Holy Ghost"—is used in an exchange outside of worship and in a counter-cultural and redemptive way. It glances off the ears of the two guests, but to the daughter, this expression becomes a catalyst for inner transformation.

If it is true that the language of worship can ripple out into the world to provide a new way of speaking and naming, it is also true that certain ways of talking in the world get us ready for worship. When a maternity nurse hands a newborn baby to its mother and the mother exclaims in joy and wonder and sheer amazement, she is trying out the kind of awestruck language of praise that will find its ultimate goal in the hymns and prayers of worship. When an immigrant raises his hand and takes the oath of citizenship or a woman places her hand on the Bible in a courtroom and pledges to be a truthful witness, these people are rehearsing the language of commitment, promise-making, and solemn devotion that will come to culmination in the vows, creeds, and promises of worship. When a man grabbing a quick sandwich in a crowded deli at lunchtime notices another man searching in vain for a vacant table and points to the empty chair at his own, saying, "Won't you join me?" he is working his way toward the language of welcome and hospitality to the stranger that reverberates most profoundly at the Lord's Table. When a married couple, over the years of weaving the rhythms of one life into those of another, learn to speak words of affirmation and support, they are preparing themselves to give and receive the blessings pronounced most firmly in worship.

The Truth, the Whole Truth, and Nothing but the Truth

Diane Komp, a pediatric oncologist, tells the of the time, early in her practice of medicine, when she was treating a little girl named Anna for leukemia. This was back in the days when the recovery rate was woefully low, and though Anna had gone in and out of remission many times, by the age of seven she was facing the end. At Anna's side at the last were her parents, a hospital chaplain who favored psychology over theology, and Komp herself, who at the time would have described herself as a "pragmatic post-Christian agnostic." Komp writes, "Before she died [Anna] mustered the final energy to sit up in her hospital bed and say: 'The angels—they're so beautiful! Mommy, can you see them? Do you hear their singing? I've never heard such beautiful singing!' Then she lay back on her pillow and died."

Anna's parents reacted "as if they had been given the most precious gift in the world." The hospital chaplain quickly left the room, leaving the agnostic Komp alone with the grieving Christian family. "Together we contemplated a spiritual mystery that transcended our understanding and experience. For weeks to follow, the thought that stuck in my head was: Have I found a reliable witness?"[12]

One of the many remarkable features of this experience is the response of Komp herself: she wonders if she has found a "reliable witness." What she means, I think, is that as an agnostic, one who questions and doubts, quests and criticizes, she was in search of someone who would tell her the truth about the depths of life, the truth about the experience of the holy, the truth finally about God. The child's words bore witness to "a spiritual mystery that transcended our understanding and experience," and Komp wonders if this child could be a teller of truth, a "reliable witness."

Indeed, the very pattern of a service of Christian worship can serve as a kind of catalogue of the ways in which our faith comes to expression in everyday speech. For example, many worship services end with a blessing or a benediction, something like the familiar words "The grace of the Lord Jesus Christ, the love of God, and the communion of the Holy Spirit be with you all." This blessing symbolizes a word from God to the people as they depart from worship that announces God's intention to be constantly with them and to work for good in their lives. The blessing, or benediction, finds many echoes outside of worship. When a young couple, for instance, informs their families that they plan to get married, there is a sense in which they really desire to have their families' blessing—which is more than permission to be married (indeed, few couples today ask for permission). They want a blessing, a bearing witness that assures them that it is the truth, the whole truth, and nothing but the truth that their families will support and honor their decision to marry. Such a blessing can be a healing and empowering force, and as such, it is ungirded by the deeper presence and providence of God as expressed in the benediction in worship. In short, the language of an element in worship, the blessing, ripples out into the language of family life.

Likewise, the psychologist Paul Pruyser has noted that many therapists and their clients experience a moment of awkwardness at the end of a session, at the close of the "therapeutic hour." Parting words are spoken—"We'll pursue this some more next time"—but such parting words are not entirely satisfying. Both therapist and client seem to be reaching for something else, something more, to say. They are hungering, argues Pruyser, for a benediction, words of blessing as they go their separate ways.

Other elements in worship also find their way into faithful speech outside the sanctuary, becoming part of people's witness in life. Here are some examples:

The Witness of Awe and Thanksgiving

Several elements in an act of Christian worship have to do with how mystery and holiness, the very presence of God, intrude into the midst of ordinary life, provoking wonder, awe, praise, and thankfulness. When worship begins with the words "Make a joyful noise to the Lord all the earth; worship the Lord with gladness," the daily treadmill has been disrupted by the presence of the holy, and the congregation responds with exclamations and hymns of wonder and praise. When

Christians gather around the table for the Lord's Supper, the Eucharist, they do so with words of thanksgiving to God, who created the world, reached out in Jesus Christ to save a wayward and broken humanity, and sustains the world every day through the Spirit. Bearing witness in the world means in part, then, discerning, describing, and giving thanks for the holiness that lies all around us, the God who has given us great gifts in the past and continues to do so.

Sometimes this bearing witness through awe and thanksgiving takes the form of words of praise, wonder, and thanks to God uttered in the course of the day. A table blessing is an echo of the thanksgiving recited at the Eucharist. Words of awe, praise, and thanks to God for health and safety, for the birth of a child, for meaning found in suffering, for the beauty of a sunset or the power of a storm, and the many other epiphanies of the day are versions "out there" in the world of the hymns and psalms of wonder uttered "in here" in worship.

In his last days, former President Harry S Truman would take a morning walk every day, often with his friend Thomas Melton, pastor of a local church. Their path would take them past an enormous ginkgo, one of the most beautiful and impressive trees in town. Truman would routinely walk over to the tree and speak to it. Years later, after Truman's death, someone asked Melton what Truman said to the tree. "He would say, 'You're doing a good job.'"[13] "You're doing a good job" was, in its own way, Truman's hymn of praise to the creation. Truman was employing on his daily walk something of the same discernment and expressing something of the same praise for the Creator and the creation that he was accustomed to singing and praying on Sunday mornings, the words of worship rippling out into faithful witness in life.

The Witness About Sin and Forgiveness

In worship, people confess their sins, speaking truthful words about the many ways that we have harmed ourselves and others and fought against God—even in our best moments. Sometimes these words of penitence, these "true confessions," are seen as gloomy, even morbid, a wallowing in self-guilt. It is important to understand, though, that confession of sin in worship takes place within the context of a merciful relationship with God—not the relationship of a judge to the accused, a jailer to a criminal, or even a stern teacher to a delinquent student, but as a loving parent to a beloved child. Confession of sin happens not in fear but in trust, and its purpose is not punishment but self-awareness, deep and honest relationship, and healing forgiveness. For every word of confession in worship, there is an assurance of pardon. For every honest admission of warfare against God, neighbor, and self, there is the announcement that "the peace of the Lord Jesus Christ be with you."

What is required in confession of sin? First, there is the courage of memory. In the face of destructiveness and cruelty, especially our own, the tendency is to hide the truth, even from ourselves. The familiar courtroom dodge of a faulty witness, "I can't remember," is echoed in all of our experience—"I can't remember" or perhaps more accurately "I refuse to remember." When Christians confess their sins, they are modeling ways of courageous memory and speech to be employed outside the sanctuary as well.

In an essay on the practice of testimony, the theologian Rebecca Chopp tells of Anna Akhmatova, a poet well known in the Soviet Union despite the fact that her poetry was banned for most of her life. In the poem "Requiem," Akhmatova tells about the political imprisonment of her son and of her long days standing with the other mothers and relatives outside the prison. In a prologue to this poem, Akhmatova writes:

> In the terrible years of the Yezhov terror I spent seventeen months waiting in line outside the prison in Leningrad. One day somebody in the crowd identified me. Standing behind me was a woman, with lips blue from the cold, who had, of course, never heard me called by name before. Now she stared out of the torpor common to us all and asked me in a whisper (everyone whispered there):
> "Can you describe this?"
> And I said, "I can." Then something like a smile passed fleetingly over what had once been her face.[14]

There are good reasons why nations do not choose to remember atrocities, why corporate executives do not recall racist policies in employment, why all of us bury the unpleasant past behind words of concealment. As Janet Malcolm notes in her book *In the Freud Archives,* "We are all perpetually smoothing and rearranging reality to conform to our wishes; we lie to others and ourselves constantly, unthinkingly. When occasionally—and not by dint of our own efforts but under the pressure of external events—we are forced to see things as they are, we are like naked people in a storm."[15] Indeed, true memory, and therefore honest confession, can take place only when we know that we are finally not "naked people in a storm" but children opening our lives to the parent who cherishes us and who has the desire to forgive and to restore.

Christians who have the courage, then, to name our public sins, to tell the truth about greed in business, negligence in the public welfare, cruelty in the social fabric, are bearing witness. Christians who are able to speak honestly with their spouses, their children, their friends, and others about the broken places in relationships are bearing witness. Christians who have the faithful courage to look deeply within and to confess that "not all is well with me" are bearing witness. But the process does not stop with confession, for Christians have discovered in the "language school" of worship that confession moves toward forgiveness and reconciliation, with God and neighbor. Thus Christians who speak out for fair housing and humane prisons and a just society and peace among the nations are also bearing witness, as are those who say tender words of mercy and pardon to their children and their spouses and their neighbors.

The Witness of Human Worth and Work

People come into worship from a world that tells them every day that they are in danger of losing their value and dignity. How much do you make? What do you do for a living? How many people do you supervise? How well did you do on the SAT? What was your grade on the history test? What neighborhood do you live in? What do you drive? What do you wear? These are the kinds of questions asked in the culture to determine human worth, and they show how fragile our place in society is. A sudden downturn in the market, a "no" from an admissions committee, an illness that puts us out of work—and suddenly we slip in the world's eyes.

When we enter the sanctuary for worship, though, we hear another word, a word that runs completely counter to the message of the culture:

> You are a chosen race, a royal priesthood, a holy nation, God's own people, in order that you may proclaim the mighty acts of him who called you out of darkness into his marvelous light. Once you were no people, but now you are God's people.
> (1 PETER 2:9–10)

This identity as God's people is announced in the words of worship—in Scripture and sermon and baptism and commission—and no standardized test, no downturn in the economy, no circumstance of life can take it away. This gift of worth and purpose spills out of the sanctuary into words of affirmation and dignity in the street. The late Howard Thurman, who was dean of the chapel at Boston University, the first African American professor at that institution, and a mentor and counselor to the leaders of the civil rights movement, attributed much of his own sense of dignity and vocation to his grandmother, a former slave, who repeated to her young grandson a message she had heard in worship. Over and over she told him, "You are *somebody!*" She was bearing witness to her grandson of a truth she heard in church.

Once when traveling through the South in the 1950s, Thurman and his family stopped to rest for a few moments at a park along the highway. His daughters immediately spotted a swing set on a playground in the park and pulled their father toward it to swing. They couldn't read the sign that warned that this playground was for "whites only by state law." Sadly but patiently, Thurman told his little girls that they could not play there and explained why. This was their first real encounter with the cruelty of racism, and they instantly burst into tears. So, much as his grandmother had done when he was a child, Thurman gathered his children into a warm embrace and said to them, "Listen, you little girls are somebody. In fact, you are so important and so valuable to God and so powerful that it takes the governor, the lieutenant governor, and the whole state police force to keep you little girls off those swings!" Here the promise first made in worship that God's people are "a chosen race, a royal priesthood, a holy nation" reverberates though the generations to affirm the dignity and value of these children whose sense of worth is threatened by the evil in the human heart.

A somewhat similar testimony about human worth was reported many years ago in the *Village Voice*. The great actress Dorothy Maguire was appearing on Broadway in Tennessee Williams's play *The Night of the Iguana*. Just before curtain time on a Friday night, the theater was disturbed by the shrill voice of a woman in the audience shouting, "Start the show! Start the show! I want to see Dorothy Maguire!" The woman was clearly emotionally disturbed, but after a moment of shocked silence, some in the theater began to turn on her. "Listen, you old bag, get out!" someone heckled. "Throw her out! Start the show!" another jeered. The house manager came to try and reason with the woman, but she pulled away, shrieking, "All I want to see is Dorothy Maguire; then I'll leave."

Suddenly, through the part in the curtains, Miss Maguire herself appeared. She crossed the stage and walked calmly over to the disturbed woman. She spoke quietly to her and then hugged her. The woman, who had recoiled whenever anyone else had touched her, drew close to Miss Maguire, got up from her seat, and together they walked toward the exit. Before they left the theater, Miss Maguire paused and turned to the audience. With grace and kindness, she announced, "I'd like to introduce another fellow human being."[16] This was testimony—a bearing witness—to a truth about this woman that no emotional illness or any abuse from others could take away. Dorothy Maguire was a reliable public witness to a promise proclaimed in worship: this was a child of God, a fellow human being.

THE END OF WORSHIP

In the traditional Roman Catholic Mass, the last words of the service were spoken by the deacon: *"Ite, missa est,"* which means "Go, you are dismissed" or, even more literally, "Go, you are sent." The Latin word for *send* has the same root as the word *mission.* So when the blessing has been pronounced, the last strains of the postlude are dying out, and we are gathering our coats and purses to leave the church, we are to think of ourselves as missionaries, as those who are sent. What are we sent to do? To be witnesses. How are we to do that? In listening, in telling the truth and in hearing honest secrets, in words of awe and wonder and in attending to the heartfelt words of others, we bear witness to God, whose Word we have encountered in worship, and to Christ, the Word become flesh (John 1:1, 14). Where are we to go? To the world, of course, and for most of us, the world is not a mission field in some distant land but an ordinary place—a home, an office, a school—and the missionary witness begins on Monday morning when the alarm clock sounds.

Part Two

TALKING THROUGH THE DAY

Chapter 4

FIRST LIGHT

The alarm clock sounds; the first pale light of morning glows around the window shade, and the day begins. This new day is mostly a day like any other. We will rouse ourselves from bed and set about the usual morning rituals. The grooves are well worn, the patterns firmly set. We will squeeze the same amount of toothpaste onto the brush, fill the coffeemaker to the usual level, pour out the customary bowl of raisin bran, comb through the paper favorite section first, check the weather, commute along the same routes, encounter the same people, go through this day on autopilot.

And yet there is something about this new day, any new day, every new day, that promises a fresh start, the prospect of something new. In the city where I live, the host of a weekend hunting and fishing radio program begins his show by opening the microphone at 4:00 A.M. and shouting zestfully, "Goood morning! Welcome to a brand-new, completely unused Saturdaaaay!" Trumpeted into the predawn darkness, this announcement startles, even jars, but it nonetheless carries the ring of truth. Every dawn does bring a brand-new, completely unused day. Every fresh day announces the chance for a new beginning, the hope of an unspoiled start, the possibility that new and stronger walls can be built on yesterday's foundation, that old wrongs can be set right, that unexpected winds and fresh surprises may blow through the day. When the alarm clock goes off and we rub the sleep out of our eyes, we are not merely struggling out of bed to start the day's routine; we are standing with one foot in the middle of history, where yesterday's realities are still waiting to be faced, and with the other foot in the Garden of Eden on the very first day of creation, full of fresh possibility. The hymn has it right: "Morning has broken, like the first morning. . . . God's re-creation of the new day!"

THIS IS THE DAY

So what do we do on the first day of creation? How do we start each new day? Many mornings, my wife and I will say to each other over the first cup of coffee, "What do you have to do today?" This is, of course, a question about obligation. We have jobs. We have responsibilities. We have commitments. We have schedules. A new day has dawned, but yesterday's obligations are present in our memory, in our Palm Pilots, on the calendar, and there are things that must be done, things we "have" to do.

On vacation days, however, the question changes. On lazy holidays, we do not ask, "What do you *have* to do today?" but rather "What would you *like* to do today?" This is a question about pleasure. Today we are free of the usual burdens. We sleep late, dress casually, leave our watches on the dresser, look out on an unfettered day without schedule or demands, and ask, "What would you *like* to do today?"

These two questions are not simply different ways to start the morning, of course; they are moral choices, rival ways to spend the time, in fact rival ways to live out our whole lives. Many of us feel constantly pulled between these two alternatives, between the burden of what we *have* to do today and the tantalizing freedom of what we'd *like* to do today. It seems like a struggle between duty and delight, maybe even between responsibility and selfishness. Ah, the dilemma. Should I cut loose and do what I really want to do, or should I buckle down and do what I am supposed to do?

For people of faith, however, there is a third way to put the question: not "What do I have to do?" or "What would I like to do?" but "What can I do today that would be joyful?" Beyond burden and pleasure, what could we do this day that would bring deep joy? Now this may seem like a Pollyannaish way to start the morning. Surely only Disney characters would bound out of bed and, before the first cup of coffee, wipe away the pixie dust from their eyes and exclaim, "What can we do today that would bring joy!" But as a matter of fact, the question of joy is neither naive nor falsely optimistic. To set out to live the day joyfully involves hard choices and difficult, even costly, decisions. Let's look more closely at this question of joy.

In one sense, "What can I do today that would be joyful?" is indeed a very different question from the questions of obligation and pleasure. Joy is not the same thing as obligation, nor is it the same as pleasure. On the obligation side, not every task entered in the Palm Pilot for the day is going to be joyful. Some of the things we have to do today—some meetings, some jobs, some assignments, some responsibilities—frankly can be boring, wasteful, irrelevant, demeaning, or even evil. We may have to do them, or think we do, but they are not joyful.

On the other hand, joy and pleasure are not synonyms either. Some joyful things—childbirth or working in a homeless shelter, for example—may involve more pain than pleasure, more sacrifice than selfishness. As the monk Thomas Merton once said, "Those who continue to struggle are at peace."[1] Likewise, some things that certain people may find pleasurable—for instance, chugging one more beer before getting behind the wheel of a Porsche—can end up destroying joy.

So joy is not to be equated with either obligation or pleasure. Yet joy has very much to do with both. Joy stands between obligation and pleasure, between duty and delight, and mediates between them. To find the place of joy is to stand at that spot where obligation and pleasure meet. The place of joy is where those things that delight us and give us pleasure, the things we freely choose ("What would you *like* to do today?") and the commitments we have made and the burdens we have agreed to carry ("What do you *have* to do today?") ultimately become one and the same.

Joy sifts through our calendars and commitments, dividing the burdens that are just heavy and useless weights from the burdens that allow us and those around us to be more alive, more human. Joy interrogates our pleasures, separating those that bring momentary relief from those that point the way to deep and abiding satisfaction.

First Light

Joyfulness is about being fully human. Joyfulness is about throwing back the covers on this brand-new, completely unused day, the first day of the new creation, and choosing to be human today, choosing to be who we were created to be. Joy answers pleasure's question, "What would you like to do today?" by saying, "Today I would like to take on the commitments—the 'have to's'—that at the end of the day will have enabled me and the people around me to be more fully human."

Ironically, when we decide to live each day seeking joy, we actually discover our deepest selves by engaging in a kind of forgetting of self. We are most joyful, most our true selves, when we are least self-absorbed and most aware of others and what lies outside of our selves. As Jesus said, "For those who want to save their life will lose it, and those who lose their life for my sake will save it" (Luke 9:24). Thomas Merton, again, put it this way:

> In an age where there is much talk about "being yourself" I reserve to myself the right to forget about being myself, since in any case there is very little chance of my being anybody else. Rather, it seems to me that when one is too intent on "being himself" he runs the risk of impersonating a shadow. . . . I am accused of living in the woods like Thoreau instead of living in the desert like St. John the Baptist. All I can answer is that I am not living "like anybody." Or "unlike anybody." We all live somehow or other, and that's that. It is a compelling necessity for me to be free to embrace the necessity of my own nature.[2]

For Merton "to embrace the necessity of my own nature" was best done by not concentrating too hard on "being himself." An attorney who graduated many years ago from the law school at the university where I teach was recently honored with an alumni award for long and distinguished community service. Early in his law career, he had raised for himself the question of joy, the question of how best to be human, and, like Merton, found that this involved a kind of "forgetting of self." Instead of choosing a lucrative practice in corporate law, he devoted his law practice to representing and defending the poor, people who would not ordinarily have had access to good legal counsel. Looking back on this choice, the lawyer said, "I didn't have to get up in the morning wondering if it would be a good day. Working with the poor and trying to do well for them, it was always a good day."

Choosing to spend the day trying to be fully and joyfully human is, of course, not just a personal choice; it is a religious decision, a matter of faith. In fact, even before it is a decision, it is a response to the call of God. Our faith tells us that we cannot be fully human and cannot be truly joyful apart from God. Sometimes a Sunday morning worship service begins this way:

> This is the day that the Lord has made.
> Let us rejoice and be glad in it!
> (PSALM 118:24)

We say this in Sunday worship, but worship, as I noted earlier, is actually a dress rehearsal for the Monday-to-Saturday world. "The day that the Lord has made" is not just Sunday. The Lord made Wednesday and Friday, too. "Let us rejoice and be glad" is not just a Sunday phrase. It is what God says to us each day, and when the morning alarm interrupts our night's sleep, it is a signal to get up and to enter "God's re-creation of the new day." On Sunday, it is the worship leader who proclaims, "This is the day that the Lord has made." On Monday, it is the buzz of the alarm clock that proclaims it, and our task is to throw off the covers, to enter God's new day, and "to rejoice and be glad in it."

What gives us the deepest joy, what makes us most fully human, what frees us to "rejoice and be glad" in the day—and this is the key—is to look for places in the world where God is at work and to join in the activity of God. Whether it is piloting a plane full of passengers from Minneapolis to Chicago, teaching a class of third graders, changing the diapers on a newborn, entering data into a computer, studying for a chemistry exam, or repairing a leaky faucet, the best work in life is work that we can understand as part of what God is doing in the world. "We must work the works of him who sent me while it is day," Jesus once told his disciples (John 9:4).

So we get up in the morning and ask, "God, what are you doing out there in the world today, and how can I be a part of it?" And what is God doing in the world? We are human beings, and we cannot know everything that God is doing. But some things we do know. Surprisingly, one of the things that we do know God is doing out there in the world, something we have always known, is that God is out there *talking*.

And that brings us right into the heart of testimony. If God is talking out there in the world, then we are to be talking too. We are to talk as God talks. That is the essence of testimony.

THE CREATION: WAS IT CALLED FOR?

On the very first day of creation, God was talking. In fact, according to the Bible, God talked the creation into being. When we ask how the universe come to be, how is it that there are galaxies and suns, planets and asteroids, how is it that there are rivers and mountains, valleys and meadows, giraffes and whales, tigers and human beings, we have to have more than one answer to the question. The truth of how the universe came to be cannot be known from a single point of view. Many scientists, for example, tell us that the universe started as a "big bang," a primordial explosion flinging chunks of matter into space. When scientists speak this way, they have taken the best data that can be gathered and blended it with the best educated guesses about how these data go together and fashioned a narrative, a plausible story, of the beginnings of the universe.

As satisfying as the "big bang" theory may be, it is not the whole story of the beginnings of the universe any more than the sheer fact that a person was formed by the union of a sperm cell and an egg is the whole story of how that person came to be. For people of faith, the universe is not just the detritus of an explosion, a haphazard heaving of planets, stars, and asteroids; it is the handiwork of God. It is not just a universe; it is a *creation*. To describe the universe as "the creation" does not pit science against faith. It simply says that if we are going to tell the whole truth of how the universe came to be, it will take more than one narrative.

According to the book of Genesis, the creation was not just a natural or random process and God was not an uninvolved bystander. God was at the very center of creation. And what was God doing? God was talking. The reader of Genesis hears God from the very beginning. The wind of God, God's breath, a divine gale, was blowing the formless void and the wild seas, and then out of the hurricane came a voice, "Let there be light," and there was light. God spoke, and the creation came to be. Scientists press their ears to instruments and, straining to listen all the way back to the beginning of time, they hear a massive explosion. Genesis listens, too, and also hears an explosion, a voice shattering the silence and talking, talking, talking. "Let there be light. Let there be seas and dry land. Let there be sun and moon and stars. Let there be plants and creatures. Let there be humankind, male and female, in our image."

Why was God talking? There was no one to hear, so why was God speaking the creation into being instead of silently, wordlessly scooping up the primeval clay and forming it into stars and moons and planets? Part of the answer is that the idea of God speaking is Bible talk for God acting. The "Word" of God is the way the Bible describes the event, the action of God.

But that's not all there is. The idea of a talking Creator is a apt metaphor because when God acts, there is always an implied R.S.V.P. When God acts, the action is speechlike in the sense that an invitation is issued, something is summoned, someone is called to, and a response is demanded. When God said, "Let there be lights in the sky," the sun and the moon sprang forth like prize hunting dogs whistled from the field. When God created human beings, the first thing God did was talk to them: "God blessed them, and God said to them, 'Be fruitful and multiply'" (Genesis 1:28). The sun and the moon, the man and the woman are not passive dollops of clay, squeezed out of a tube onto the canvas of the sky. They are God's conversation partners. When God's voice called out to them, they listened and responded. Even out of nothingness, they heard and they came forth.

In *God's Trombones,* the African American poet James Weldon Johnson imagines a old-time folk preacher setting forth the biblical creation story:

> And God stepped out on space,
> And he looked around and said:
> I'm lonely—
> I'll make me a world.[3]

What if the old preacher had it right about God and loneliness? What if God did not create the world on a whim or a dare or simply because he could do whatever he pleased, a dramatic and showy exercise of divine power, but because God desired companionship? What if God created the world not just so there would be the thrill of Niagara Falls, the dizzying heights of the Himalayas, or the stark beauty of the Sahara but so there would be an ear to hear and a voice to respond? What if the old preacher had it right and God stepped out into space and shouted the creative Word across the canyon of ageless silence yearning this time for something more than an echo but instead a voice bravely answering back, "Here I am"?

When I misbehaved as a child, my mother would sometimes say, "Now that was uncalled for!" A strange phrase, *uncalled for,* as if something about being good had to be summoned, as if something about *me,* the real me, the me I was supposed to be, wasn't just there already formed but had to be called for. Maybe my mother said "uncalled for" because that's the way mothers of her generation spoke, or maybe mothers spoke that way because of some deep memory of childbirth. When I was born, she and my father turned to each other, as mothers and fathers for generations have done, and said, "What shall we call this one? Let's call him 'Thomas.'" Forget for a moment all the long debates about nature and nurture; in their naming, they were summoning the me who was not yet, summoning in me and from me all of their deepest hopes, calling me to come forth to receive their very best gifts, calling me to leave my isolation and to come and be with them, because it is not good for human beings to be alone. I was not just born; I was *called for,* and so were you.

Likewise, according to Genesis, the whole creation is called for. God did not create the world in silence, like some quiet potter in the basement wordlessly throwing blobs of clay on a wheel. Rather, God spoke, summoning into being what did not yet exist. God shouted above the howl of the winds raging over the waters, calling loudly, "Let there be light!" and there was light. God whispered in the secret recesses of the divine life, saying softly, "Let us make humankind in our image," and there were human beings in God's very own likeness. Sky and sea, sun and moon, tree and fruit, wild animal and human being—they did not just appear; they were *called for.*

The Christian novelist Frederick Buechner points out that the beginning of each new day is a recapitulation of this story of creation, a retelling of the time when God's creative voice went calling:

> Darkness was upon the face of the deep, and God said "Let there be light." Darkness laps my sleeping face like a tide, and God says, "Let there be Buechner." Why not? Out of the primeval chaos of sleep he calls me to be a life again. . . . He calls me to be this rather than that; he calls me to be here rather than there; he calls me to be now rather than then. . . . Waking into the new day, we are all of us Adam on the morning of creation, and the world is ours to name.[4]

DEEP CALLS TO DEEP

So the first word that is spoken each new day comes from God. God calls to each of us, calls us from sleep, calls us to get up and be human, to live toward joy, to put one foot in front of the other this day as one who belongs to God. How do we do this? There are many ways and places, of course, to express our humanity, our calling, throughout the day, but among the first human acts we do each day is to imitate God by opening our mouths and speaking. God speaks the creation into being, and we respond to God's voice with our own.

Maybe the first words we will speak are a prayer. Perhaps we begin the day by speaking back to God, who has spoken us into life.

First Light

"When the thought of thee wakes in our hearts," prayed Kierkegaard at the beginning of the day, "let it not awaken like a frightened bird that flies about in dismay, but like a child waking from its sleep with a heavenly smile."[5] Maybe we begin the day by bowing our heads or bending our knees and confessing that we are not alone here in Eden.

Or maybe our morning prayer is simpler than Kierkegaard's, a word cried out to God as we shuffle through the closet looking for something to wear or a whispered "Give me strength today, O Lord" as we put the Pop Tart in the toaster.

Prayer is expression, of course, speaking to God from the bottoms of our hearts, but it is also a spiritual discipline. Like my cross-country runner stepson getting up at dawn to run seven miles with his teammates, Christians have learned over the centuries some good prayer exercises and disciplines. Brevity, for example. "When you are praying, do not heap up empty phrases," said Jesus (Matthew 6:7), and Martin Luther agreed. "The fewer the words, the better the prayer," said Luther. The writer Anne Lamott, a disarmingly candid Christian, once said that all of her praying could be basically boiled down to two phrases, either "Thank you! Thank you!" or "Help me! Help me!"[6]

Another reformer, John Calvin, was bold enough to state four "rules" for prayer.[7] In paraphrased form, they are something like this:

1. Remember, when you pray, that you are talking with God, so focus your heart and mind accordingly. This does not mean, by the way, pretending not to have any anxiety about life. In fact, anxiety can actually increase the fervor of prayer.
2. Don't make the mistake of thinking that God loves prayer noises. God is no more fond of windy prayer phrases and pompous piety than you are. When you pray, do so with sincerity. Say what you really feel, ask for what you truly need, and pray with ardent desire.
3. Holier-than-thou people turn God off. Prayer is about emptying ourselves, not puffing ourselves up. Praying well is a matter of humility before God, not vainly patting ourselves on the

back for being such good, prayerful people. Go to God as a child does to a loving parent—confidently, simply, and humbly.

4. Expect your prayers to be answered. The answers may not come in the form you thought, but God is a good and loving parent who will faithfully give you all that you ask in faith and genuinely need.

In the musical *Fiddler on the Roof,* Tevye, a poor Jewish milkman in a small Russian village, is depicted as a man of prayer. He prays at the synagogue and he prays at the Sabbath table, but mainly he prays as he goes about his everyday life. He talks to God as freely and honestly as he would talk to any trusted friend. Tevye asks God why, in God's great wisdom, it was necessary that he be the father of five daughters and no sons. Tevye says he loves his daughters . . . "but five?" Tevye wishes he were not so poor, and he asks God, almost teasingly, if it would have disturbed some great divine plan if Tevye could have been rich. In his free-flowing, honest speaking to God, his conversation with God punctuating the day, Tevye is a picture of what Paul meant when he urged Christians to "pray without ceasing" (1 Thessalonians 5:17).

IT IS NOT GOOD THAT HUMANITY SHOULD BE ALONE

If our first thoughts and words of the new day are prayerfully directed to God, we soon seek out companionship in other people. In the Garden of Eden, Adam was intrigued by the lush plants and the delightful animals, but he was not fully satisfied. He desired that there be another creature like himself, bone of his bone and flesh of his flesh.

We have the same desire. Go through any shopping mall or airport and notice how many people are walking along jabbering into cell phones. What are all these conversations about? Sometimes they involve matters of consequence, but mainly they consist of phrases like "Whasup?" or "I'm here. We just landed." In other words, they are less about information and more a calling out to other creatures in the

Garden. "Hello. I'm here. Are you there? Bone of my bone and flesh of my flesh?" In the first light of each new day, we call out to God, and then we call out for communion with others.

In the maximum-security section of the county lockup in my town, there is a heavy metal wall with tiny holes drilled in it. When someone visits a prisoner, the visitor sits on one side of the wall, the prisoner on the other, and conversation takes place through the little holes in the wall. Around the holes, the paint has been worn away where countless people have pressed their faces to the wall, even kissed it, trying to get as close as possible to the one on the other side. In spite of the walls that often divide us, we hunger for voice of the other, desire to be in the other's company, and call out to the other: "Hello. I'm here. Are you there? Bone of my bone and flesh of my flesh?"

When Christians call out to others, faithful speech is more than "Whasup?" Testimony is more than "Hey, I'm here. I've landed"— but what is it? There is an ancient custom in Christian worship that as the believers gather around the Lord's table, they greet each other with the kiss of peace. Today many worship services include a form of this called "the passing of the peace," in which worshipers turn to take the hand of the neighbor and say, "The peace of Christ be with you." The neighbor responds, "And also with you."

In a way, all testimony, all Christian speaking with others, could be summed up in those words, "The peace of Christ be with you," and all hope for community could be expressed in the reply, "And also with you." To offer Christ's peace to another is to offer God's great *shalom,* the hope that all will truly be well. God promises that one day God will fully dwell with all humans and that "God will wipe away every tear from their eyes. Death will be no more; mourning and crying and pain will be no more" (Revelation 21:3–4). This is God's peace; this is the deepest hope of the human heart; this is the peace the angels sang in the night sky over Bethlehem when Jesus was born. True testimony is an invitation to the other to share that hope and to live even now in that great peace: "The peace of Christ be with you."

Prayer is a sign of that peace, and this means that prayer is actually speech that works in two directions. First, to pray is to engage in conversation with God, but second, prayer is also a witness, a testimony. When the world sees us at prayer, it sees a peace sign. Prayer is a sign that a cease-fire has been declared in the warfare of human beings against God. God has made peace with us, and we can talk.

Prayer as testimony played a profound role in the life of Dorothy Day, the founder of the Catholic Worker community and a Christian whose deep faith and commitment to the downtrodden was a powerful influence on many others. In the 1930s, when her Catholic Worker houses began providing shelter to the homeless, she was sharply criticized. People said she was caring for drunkards and drifters and not for the "deserving poor." "How long are you going to let these people stay in your homes?" she was asked.

"We let them stay forever," she replied fiercely. "They live with us, they die with us, and we give them a Christian burial. We pray for them after they are dead. Once they are taken in, they become members of the family. Or rather they always were members of the family. They are our brothers and sisters in Christ."[8]

When she described what led her to Christianity and to her sense of calling, Dorothy Day often cited an experience early in her life. As a little girl living in Chicago, she went looking for a friend who lived next door. She found that the door to her friend's apartment was open, so she went in. She saw that the breakfast dishes had been washed and stacked beside the sink. Then she discovered her friend's mother, Mrs. Barrett, kneeling on the floor saying her prayers. When Mrs. Barrett heard Dorothy, she stopped praying long enough to tell her that her friend had gone to the store. Then she returned to her prayers. Years later, Dorothy Day remembered, "I felt a burst of love toward Mrs. Barrett that I've never forgotten."

One of Day's biographers has written that this encounter with Mrs. Barrett saying her morning prayers was "one of the early moments that she felt a first encounter with the transcendent. This sense that there was more to life became an irresistible call beckoning her and ultimately leading her into the Church."[9] Day herself once said that "worship, adoration, thanksgiving, supplication . . . were the noblest acts of which we are capable in this life."[10]

Faithful speech that seeks peace and communion with others is not always in the form of prayer. Sometimes it does not even sound very religious. Sometimes Christian testimony sounds less like holy talk and more like this: "Honey, would you like some coffee?" And the response comes: "That would be great. Just half a cup. Do you mind?" "Time to get ready for school," we call to our children as we shake them from sleep, and they say in return, "Already?"

Why do I say this is *religious* speech? It's just the sound of morning chatter, the white noise of human beings starting the day. Nothing from the Bible is quoted. The name of God may not even be said. Why do I call it testimony? Because we are using speech to do what God is doing in the world, calling out to others, seeking to bridge the lonely gap and to form peaceful, reconciled communion with others. As human beings created in God's image and summoned to life, we are calling out to others as God called out to us. Why? Because "it is not good that humanity should be alone." As Buechner says, "Another life—alive, like you, by the giddy grace of God—reaches across the light-years that separate each other from the other and touches your hand and names your name like God the Father on Michelangelo's ceiling who reaches out of the cloud and touches Adam, names Adam's flesh to holy life."[11]

Even if there is no one there, we speak, speak to the hole in life where the spouse, the child, the companion would be if there were one. We turn on the TV, hungry for the sound of another voice, hungry to speak back, hungry to make contact, hungry for communion with the other. "It is not good that humanity should be alone."

The religious educator Hubertus Halbfas once observed, "Some people just speak about children, their house and garden, supper and bed . . . , and yet their discourse is full of faith and hope, thanks and prayer."[12] For example, consider the following experience. In the middle of the night, a mother hears her child cry out in fear. She swiftly pulls on her robe, hastens to the child's bedside, and finds her child trembling in terror from a bad dream. Suddenly, the night has become for the child full of dread, every shadow a threat, every creaking rafter a danger, and the child is desperately afraid. The mother knows instinctively what to do, as mothers in all times have known. She turns on a lamp and speaks soothing comfort to her child. Perhaps she sings a song or tells a familiar story. Maybe she rocks her child in her arms

82

TESTIMONY

or gently touches the child's cheek. As her child gradually becomes calm, the mother soothingly says, "Go back to sleep. Don't be afraid. Nothing will harm you. Everything is all right."

This mother did what any good parent would do in such circumstances. She would probably be quite surprised to learn that some would consider that she was performing a religious action, engaging in religious speech, participating in a theological conversation with her child. Why *religious*? Why *theological*? After all, she simply went to her child with words of reassurance in a time of need. She did not mention God or sing a hymn or pray a prayer. She just encouraged her child not to be afraid, offering the comforting words that everything is all right. But if we think carefully about this mother's words, we follow a path in our thinking that leads to the recognition that the mother has done more than offer mere reassurance; she has in some ways—perhaps even beyond her own awareness—expressed her faith.

Notice first, as the sociologist of religion Peter Berger has pointed out, that the mother's words raise the issue of truth. Parents reassure their frightened children in the middle of the night all the time—this is very common—but, as Berger states, "this common scene raises a far from ordinary question, which introduces a religious dimension: *Is the mother lying to the child?*"[13] When parents reassure their children that everything is all right, they mean to say more, something larger, than there is no monster in the closet *tonight* or no goblin under the bed *this* time. They mean to say beyond this one night, beyond these few moments of fear, beyond this little room, that the world and life itself are to be trusted and not feared.

But is this so? Did the mother speak the truth? Is *everything* really all right? One is tempted to say no, not really. As an adult, the mother surely knows that every life has its measure of trouble, that she and her child will bear their share of suffering, that eventually she will die, so will her child, and all those whom they love. The world is full of harmful forces, and no one makes it through life untouched by evil and suffering. In the world in which all of us are born, live out our lives, and finally die, everything is definitely *not* all right. So if these universal realities of human experience are all there are, then the mother's love and words of comfort are at best tragically heroic

First Light

and at worst a gentle deception. We may, Berger notes, eventually "find ourselves in darkness, alone with the night that will swallow us up. The face of reassuring love, bending over our terror, will then be nothing except an image of merciful illusion."[14]

But this mother is not merely concocting a "loving lie." On the contrary, whether she is aware of it or not (and she may well not be), she is bearing witness to her conviction that life is more than the terrors that assail human beings here and now, more than the suffering and pain, destruction and death that are the fate of all of us. These things do happen to people—she knows that—but they are not the only realities, not even the most important ones. Her word that "everything is all right" goes beyond the immediate situation to imply something she believes about reality as such, that finally and ultimately there is a trustworthiness about the universe and its Lord that allows for peaceful sleep at night and courageous living in the day. Regarding adult integrity, which includes religious faith, Erik Erikson observed, "Healthy children will not fear life if their elders have integrity enough not to fear death."[15] Her words of comfort to her child spring from parental love, but she is able to speak them because of her faith in a world "in which love is not annihilated in death, and . . . the trust in the power of love to banish chaos is justified."[16]

In the same way, when at the day's first light we venture from our rooms, venture from our homes, venture out into the world and call out to another in the ordinary speech of human communion, we have begun our testimony to the ways of God. Language is powerful. Words can bless, and words can curse. Words can build up, and words can destroy. Words can create relationships of love and trust, and words can destroy another's reputation. Whenever we use our words to join in the activity of God in the world—to form community, to heal, to forgive, to set things right—we are bearing faithful witness to God.

Many years ago, the theologian Paul Tillich preached a famous and often-quoted sermon called "You Are Accepted." In this sermon, Tillich spoke about the theological ideas of grace, forgiveness, and justification by faith in more familiar, nontheological language—as ac-

TESTIMONY

ceptance. In one particularly moving section of the sermon, Tillich said:

> Sometimes at that moment a wave of light breaks into our darkness, and it is as though a voice were saying: You are accepted. You are accepted, accepted by that which is greater than you, and the name of which you do not know. Do not ask for the name now; perhaps you will find it later. Do not try to do anything now; perhaps later you will do much. Do not seek for anything; do not perform anything; do not intend anything. Simply accept the fact that you are accepted![17]

When "You Are Accepted" appeared in a published collection of Tillich's sermons, it was inspiring to a whole generation of college students, including David Bartlett, a graduate of Yale Divinity School who is now on the faculty there. However, Bartlett reports that when he first got to Yale, he discovered that Tillich's sermon was not very well accepted by some members of the Yale faculty. Tillich, claimed his critics, hadn't been theological enough in his language. He had watered down Pauline theology, substituting the existential concept of "acceptance" for the theological doctrine of justification by faith.

Bartlett understands this criticism, but he had the occasion to wonder whether it was fully on target when he was watching a television program about communicating with autistic children. A reporter on the show was interviewing a construction worker, the father of an autistic child. This man, Bartlett guesses, had never read Tillich's sermon. Nevertheless, the father, Bartlett wrote, was saying "how much his son felt cut off, estranged, alienated, disconnected. 'What is it you would wish for your son?' the reporter asked. The father could hardly speak. Then finally, 'I just want him to be accepted.'"[18]

In her memoir *The Whisper Test,* Mary Ann Bird tells of the power of words of acceptance in her own life. She was born with multiple birth defects: deaf in one ear, a cleft palate, a disfigured face, a crooked nose, lopsided feet. As a child, Mary Ann suffered not only the physical impairments but also the emotional damage inflicted by other children. "Oh, Mary Ann," her classmates would say, "what happened to your lip?"

"I cut it on a piece of glass," she would lie.

One of the worst experiences at school, she reported, was the day of the annual hearing test. The teacher would call each child to her desk, and the child would cover first one ear, and then the other. The teacher would whisper something to the child like "The sky is blue" or "You have new shoes." This was "the whisper test"; if the teacher's phrase was heard and repeated, the child passed the test. To avoid the humiliation of failure, Mary Ann would always cheat on the test, secretly cupping her hand over her one good ear so that she could still hear what the teacher said.

One year Mary Ann was in the class of Miss Leonard, one of the most beloved teachers in the school. Every student, including Mary Ann, wanted to be noticed by her, wanted to be her pet. Then came the day of the dreaded hearing test. When her turn came, Mary Ann was called to the teacher's desk. As Mary Ann cupped her hand over her good ear, Miss Leonard leaned forward to whisper. "I waited for those words," Mary Ann wrote, "which God must have put into her mouth, those seven words which changed my life." Miss Leonard did not say "The sky is blue" or "You have new shoes." What she whispered was "I wish you were my little girl." Mary Ann went on to become a teacher herself, a person of inner beauty and great kindness.[19]

Sometimes the most faithful testimony doesn't sound very religious. Sometimes a teacher's whisper of encouragement, a word of greeting spoken over the top of a newspaper and a cup of coffee or on an elevator or a subway, communicates, as Tillich claimed, "you are accepted, accepted by that which is greater than you, and the name of which you do not know." Whenever we use our words to join in the activity of God in the world—to form community, to heal, to forgive, to set things right—we are bearing faithful witness to God.

IN THE NAME OF GOD

Although it is true that not all testimony speaks directly of God, sooner or later Christians will get around to explicit God talk. Faithful Christian speech does what God is doing in the world. It establishes communion, proclaims peace and acceptance, and sets things right, but it also tells the truth about the God whose light shines in every corner of human existence.

Late in her life, Dorothy Day said, "If I have achieved anything in my life, it is because I have not been embarrassed to talk about God."[20] Christians are not embarrassed to talk about God. This does not mean that all Christians are polished theologians or can spin out articulate descriptions of the ways of God. What it does mean is that Christians don't keep their God talk closed up in the sanctuary, locked behind the doors of the church. Christians are bold to name God, thank God, praise God, cry out to God, and share the news of God in public places.

Some years ago, a friend of mine was admitted to the hospital with severe pain in his stomach. It turned out to be a massive blockage in his small intestine, and emergency surgery was necessary. After the surgery, he spent a restless and pain-filled night in his hospital bed. At the close of this seemingly endless night, just as the sun was coming up, a nurse he had not seen before, a middle-aged woman, entered his room and began to check his vital signs. "How are you?" she asked tenderly.

Gazing out the window at the streak of sunlight, my friend answered, "It looks like it might be a good day."

"Honey," she said, "every day that the Lord made is a good day. We will rejoice and be glad in it."

My friend, a Christian, recognized this as a line from the Bible, and reaching into his memory, he recited a few words of another Bible verse. The nurse recognized the verse and whispered the last few words with him. Then she recited another Bible verse. As the nurse filled the water pitcher and smoothed the blanket, these two people in a hospital room spoke Bible verses back and forth, some from the Psalms, some from the Gospels. "One of us would start a verse and the other would take up the refrain and finish it," wrote my friend. "It . . . made me forget the pain and discomfort for a while."[21]

HEADING OUT THE DOOR AND INTO THE WORLD

At the first light of day, we begin to talk. We talk to God because God has first spoken to us. And we talk to other people. We talk to others because the way God made us, it is not good for us to be alone. We try to shape our words so that they will invite others to be our companions, so that they will be full of Christ's peace.

But now the day has begun. Breakfast is over, and we are dressed and ready for the day. We go out now to teach, to run machines, to sell insurance, to drive trucks, to clean houses, to raise children, to manage accounts, to coach, to do many things. Some of us will go out to fight the traffic. Others of us will go out by staying at home to care for others. Still others, confined to bed or even prison, will go out only through our prayers. However we go out, as Christians we are not just employees or commuters or citizens; we are *witnesses,* and what we will do in the world is testimony.

A version of the Bible used by some Christians has a book called Sirach. This book imagines ordinary people, people like potters, at work. These people, says Sirach, are not kings or great leaders. Nobody expects them to be able to quote huge sections of the Bible or to spout wise sayings. And yet without them, the city would not be livable. Without what they do, human society could not be sustained. "They keep stable the fabric of the world," says Sirach, "and their prayer is in the practice of their trade" (Sirach 38:34).

The first light of day has now warmed into a full sun, and it is time to go to work.

Chapter 5

WALKING THE WALK, TALKING THE TALK

When the time comes to begin the workday, Christians head out to do mostly what others do—teach school, install ductwork, sell refrigerators, balance books, set broken bones, wait on tables, operate computers, and run cash registers. Even Christians who do not have paying jobs still engage the world in other ways. They volunteer at the hospital, visit neighbors, take care of children, call friends on the phone, and go to the market. When Christians open the front door and venture out to do their daily tasks, they do not leave their faith at home, of course, and this can make the day very complicated. Sometimes, frankly, the commands of Jesus and the demands of life—a job, a social setting, or a relationship—are in tension, if not outright conflict, and the workaday life of Christians is filled with a thousand moral dilemmas.

Not the least of these has to do with how Christians should talk out in the world. In almost every job, every place of service, Christians will spend the day talking to other people. They will talk to coworkers, customers, clients, patients, and students. How should they talk in the workaday world? Most of the time this talk will not be overtly religious—being a Christian bank teller does not mean handing Bible verses to the customers along with their deposit slips.

In *The Monday Connection,* his book about the interaction of faith and the world of work, William Diehl tells about Helen, the

89

"office evangelist." Helen was a supervisor of clerical staff in a district office of Bethlehem Steel. She had a glass-enclosed private office overlooking the staff room, and prominent on her desk was a Bible. Whenever Helen heard about any of her employees having a personal problem, she would invite them into her office, close the door, and in full view of the whole staff, read the Bible to them. Helen was a caring, soft-spoken person, and she had every intention of doing good. She genuinely believed that the answers to all of her employees' problems could be found in Scripture, and her Bible-reading stints were exercises in compassion. But her attempt to be a Christian witness was largely counterproductive, simply stirring up resentment among her staff. Not only did they object to Helen's pressing her religious convictions upon them, but they also felt exposed having the Bible read to them in the view of others. Office conversation became much more guarded as the employees feared that any mention of a personal issue would land them in one of Helen's Scripture sessions. Finally, management had to step in to moderate Helen's activities.[1]

Christians should be, as Jesus said, "wise as serpents and innocent as doves" (Matthew 10:16). On the "innocent as doves" side, Christians should speak of their faith as freely as they breathe. The fact that honest God talk is taboo in some social settings is not a sign that it is irrelevant but, to the contrary, an indication of how powerfully important it is. On the "wise as serpents" side, because honest God talk is so potent, Christians should choose well the times, places, and means for speaking. Sometimes, as in the case of the "office evangelist," what seems like honest sharing of the faith can push others away or give them a sense of being manipulated. Also, as I have noted before, authentic God talk does not always depend on the use of explicitly religious words. Read, for example, the story of Jesus and the woman who was caught in adultery (John 8:1–11). Jesus does not mention God once in this story, but what he says is clearly faithful speech. He stops the woman's accusers in their tracks by saying, "Let anyone among you who is without sin be the first to throw a stone at her," and he offers grace to the woman by saying, "Neither do I condemn you. Go your way, and from now on do not sin again." His words of challenge, forgiveness, and courageous compassion are full of the energy of God. He does not say the word *God,* but his words are God's words.

So even though Christian talk is not necessarily always religious talk, it should always be faithful talk. That is, whatever we say in the world should be shaped by our faith. Earlier, in Chapter Two, I presented the portrait of Christians as witnesses. We are called to go out into the world and give testimony, to tell the truth. Out there in the world, talking to all sorts of people in all kinds of settings, Christians want to tell the truth, the whole truth, and nothing but the truth.

Just tell the truth. That sounds simple enough, but, of course, it is not. In our culture, it is the truth, after all, that is often most imperiled.

SPIN CONTROL

In the comedy film *Crazy People,* Dudley Moore plays the part of Emory Leeson, an advertising executive who comes up one day with an outrageous idea: telling the truth. "Let's face it," Emory tells a coworker, "you and I lie for a living." So, daring to buck the trend, Emory begins to draft copy for ruthlessly honest ads. Instead of a thousand subtle deceptions about how some product will make people happier, sexier, or richer, he says things like "Volvos: they're boxy, but they're safe" or "United Airlines: most of our passengers get there alive."

Predictably, Emory's unconventional tactics get him in hot water with his boss and, worse, raise suspicions that he has lost touch with reality. So he is packed away to a psychiatric hospital to restore his "sanity." But while he is locked up, his agency accidentally releases his ads to the public, and the results are astounding. The public is so shocked, amazed, and delighted by hearing the unvarnished truth for once, sales skyrocket.

A silly Hollywood movie? Yes, but *Crazy People* contains at least two grains of wisdom nonetheless. The first is obvious. We all hunger for the truth, and we long for a society where politicians, newscasters, car dealers, and even Madison Avenue hucksters turn off the spin and the lies. But there is a second bit of wisdom in *Crazy People,* this one less obvious. We often laugh outside at what worries us most inside. The movie gets a lot of laughs by poking fun at the world of advertising, where people lie for a living and truth-tellers are considered insane, but the audience's laughter may be a defense mechanism. It is human nature to be anxious about our constant susceptibility to lies. Not only do we hunger for the truth, but we also need people who will tell us the truth; in fact, we need such people so desperately that we are all vulnerable to half-truths and deceptions. We want to believe what other people tell us, even when our best instincts tell us to be cautious. So we use a movie like *Crazy People* to reassure ourselves that underneath it all, we are too smart to be taken in by lies and come-ons, aren't we? Others may be gullible, but not we. We are on to the game and too savvy for that. We know better.

The fact is, though, that we do not know better. Everything that matters to us—who we love, what we give our lives to, how we live—depends on words that are true and trustworthy, and we are forever vulnerable to being deceived. Sure, we are all savvy to the fact that ads often misrepresent the wares, but when the next TV commercial promises that a new pasta dish is more healthful or a new detergent more effective, we still pay attention. People may have had their hearts broken by a dozen false lovers, but chances are good that the next attractive man or woman with sincere-sounding words of love will raise their hopes anew. A person may have been passed over for promotion time and again but still cling to the next flattering word from a supervisor. Consumer experts warn us that con artists and flimflams abound, and the reason these scams repeatedly work is not that the victims are stupid but that they are human. It is very human to want to believe, very human to want to trust that the words spoken to us are true.

Indeed, we cannot live without trustworthy words, cannot be human without them. If at least some words cannot be relied on, we have no way of knowing who we are, cannot build relationships of love, and are unable to make even the most modest plans for how we shall live. So no matter how many times we get knocked over by half-truths and wholesale lies, we get right back up for the next round. If Christians commit to telling the truth, then, they are not just being nice people. They are using words in the way human beings most need to hear them.

Making the point that everyday human life depends on the reliability and truthfulness of words, the philosopher C.A.J. Coady imagines that he is traveling to a foreign city, say, Amsterdam. When his plane arrives, Coady believes he is in Amsterdam, not because he knows this for sure—he has never been to Amsterdam before—but because the pilot assures the passengers over the intercom that they are landing in Amsterdam. When he checks into his hotel, he fills out a form giving his name, date of birth, citizenship, and so on. Not only is all of this accepted as true by the desk clerk simply because Coady says it is true, but also Coady himself believes it is true. He is sure that he is named C.A.J. Coady, that he was born on such-and-such a date, and that he is so many years old not because of any concrete evidence but because others have told him that these things are true.

The next morning, when Coady wakes up, he calls the desk to get the local time, and he believes what the desk clerk says. Over breakfast, he reads a paperback about the amazing exploits of Napoleon more than 150 years before, and he believes that there was a Napoleon who was important in history, even though he has obviously not met Napoleon personally or experienced any of his exploits at first hand. The morning paper carries news of a military coup in Spain, and even though he has no way of verifying this for himself, he takes this news to be factual. After breakfast, Coady heads out of the hotel to do some sightseeing, tourist map in hand, once more trusting himself to the word of others.[2] The point is clear. In a scientific age, we may think we base our knowledge and decision making on hard evidence, but in fact we live life mainly on the basis of testimony. Everyday life is dependent on people's speaking truthful words to us.

No wonder we dream of a world where advertisers tell the truth. No wonder we hunger for public discourse to be free of deception and spin. No wonder we yearn for people to be as good as their word. No wonder, then, that when Christians put the breakfast dishes in the sink and head out into the workaday world, what they are called to do, and what the world needs most from them, is to go out there and in every arena of life to tell the truth. It is startling, often

Walking the Walk, Talking the Talk

breathtakingly refreshing, and, as *Crazy People* wryly reminds us, sometimes seemingly insane, but it is what Christian testimony is all about: telling the truth.

Telling the truth in everyday affairs may seem a simple and obvious thing to do, but it is not. The stakes are high. Lies and deceptions are not just the result of media manipulation or political maneuvering. The struggle between deception and truth lies deep in the human heart and traverses the whole span of human history. Christians know that spin control did not start yesterday on Madison Avenue or Pennsylvania Avenue; it began in the very beginning.

THE SNAKE IN THE GARDEN

The problem with words, the problem with truth and lies, the problem with honesty and spin, goes all the way back to Adam and Eve in the Garden of Eden. The Bible presents the story of the Garden of Eden as an account of what happened at the very beginning to the very first human beings. Theologically, however, the story of the Garden of Eden is a story of what happens always and to everybody.

"Where is the Garden of Eden?" a man once asked his pastor, Carlyle Marney.

"Two-fifteen Elm Street, Knoxville, Tennessee," said Marney.

"You're lying," the man scoffed. "It's supposed to be someplace in Asia."

"Well, you couldn't prove it by me," Marney said. "For there on Elm Street, when I was but a boy, I stole a quarter out of my Mama's purse and went down to the store and bought some candy and I ate it and then I was so ashamed that I came back and hid in the closet. It was there she found me and asked, 'Where are you? Why are you hiding? What have you done?'"[3]

The common view of the story of Adam and Eve is that it is a story about temptation, but it is really more a story about truth and trust. In the popular understanding, the snake slithers up to Eve and tempts her with a shiny red apple. But that is not the way the story really goes. According to the book of Genesis, the crafty serpent did not tempt Eve with an apple or anything else. In fact, the snake was not interested in apples; the snake was interested in *words*—weasel words, slippery words, ambiguous words, lying words.

Notice the serpent's opening gambit. "Did God say, 'You shall not eat from any tree in the garden'?" (Genesis 3:1). That is the first thing the serpent says to the woman, and I must admit, it is a very clever way to put the matter. "Did God say . . . ?" This is so low-key, such a smooth conversation starter, but by posing this seemingly innocent question, the serpent, for the first time in human history, has subtly raised the possibility that words might not be all that they seem. "Did God say . . . ?" The serpent doesn't call God a liar. The snake makes no charges or allegations. Instead the snake just plants a little seed of doubt in the woman's mind about words. "Did God say . . . ?"

The serpent is like a neighbor kid saying to a playmate, "Did your mother *really* say we couldn't play in the mud puddles?" The very question creates uncertainty, subtly challenges the authority and trustworthiness of words, not to mention the authority and trustworthiness of the mother. Maybe your mother meant this mud puddle but not that one. Maybe your mother meant yesterday but not today. Or maybe your mother didn't mean us at all. "Did your mother *really say* . . . ?" The question subtly suggests that maybe the mother equivocated, that maybe she said this and maybe she said that and maybe the whole thing was just a bunch of words. "Did God say . . . ?" Well, maybe God did and maybe God didn't. Any maybe words, even God's words, might be subject to spin and interpretation, might not be fully truthful. These are the implications of the serpent's seemingly harmless little question, "Did God say . . . ?"

When biblical scholars take tweezers and carefully pull apart every word of the exchange between the snake and the woman in Eden, an astonishing fact emerges. The crafty serpent cannot be caught in a flat-footed lie. The snake manages to tear apart the fabric of truth, but never once does he commit an outright deception. Everything the serpent says is "kind of true," in the same way many television commercials and product warranties and press releases are "kind of true." By the end of the conversation, however, truth has been leveled and buried. Spin control and half-truths have

Walking the Walk, Talking the Talk

undermined all trust in words, God's words and human words. Everything is now up for grabs. Do words mean what they say? Does God speak the truth? Do men and women speak the truth? Can God be trusted? Can anyone be trusted?

Eden displays the sad reality that people have turned words into word games. The cost is the loss of trust, trust between human beings, trust between us and God. We know this all too well from our everyday experience. The letter comes in the mail and what looks like a check can be seen winking through the plastic window. "Our gift for you!" it says on the envelope. Sure enough, inside is a $25 check made out to you and ready to be cashed. Why? Because, the letter says, "we want to reward you for your loyalty as a customer." On the back of the check, however, is a paragraph of small print. Endorse the check and you have unwittingly agreed to switch phone companies or signed up for insurance or subscribed to a travel magazine. "Did God say . . . ?" What started in Eden with a simple question about trust in God's words and ends up with "kind of true" words that are really lies in the mailbox. Do words mean what they say? Can words be trusted?

When former President Clinton testified before the grand jury in the Monica Lewinsky matter, one of the questioners reminded him that previous testimony had claimed there was no sex of any kind between the president and Ms. Lewinsky. That, said the questioner, "was an utterly false statement. Is that correct?"

"It depends upon what the meaning of the word *is* means," the president famously replied. "If *is* means 'is,'" Clinton went on to say, "'and never has been,' that's one thing. If it means 'there is none,' that was a completely true statement." The story of Eden goes on. "Did you say . . . ?" "Did God say . . . ?" Do words mean what they say? Do men and women speak the truth? Can we trust each other's words?

So how should Christians talk when they are out in the world? One way to put it is that Christians are called to talk to each other and to other people like Adam and Eve in the Garden of Eden before the snake tied human language into knots of double-talk. Christians are to speak in ways that can be trusted. Like everybody else, Christians will use words in a thousand ways in everyday life—talking on the phone, ordering in restaurants, making presentations to clients, counseling patients, handling complaints from customers, and swapping stories at the coffeepot, just to name a few. Christians talk in all kinds of ways and in all sorts of settings, but the number one goal in all of these contexts is to tell the truth.

One might be surprised to know that Don Flow has decided to tell the truth. Flow is a car dealer, an occupation not always famous for its straight shooting. But Flow is also a thoughtful Christian, and he has reflected deeply on the relationship between his faith and his work. He believes that God has called him to do his job in such a way that he helps create "relationships that point to the kingdom of God," and he has decided that this calls for him, among other things, to tell the truth. Flow says, "Truth-telling is the foundation for developing trust. Simply stated, we trust people we can believe in, and we believe in people who tell the truth."[4]

For Don Flow, the idea that we ought to tell the truth is not just a civic motto but an idea he learned in worship. He quotes the Gospel of John that the Word "became flesh . . . full of grace and truth" (John 1:14), and he says, "Grace and truth were the hallmarks of the Incarnate Word, and I believe they are central to pointing people to the Risen Lord."[5]

Nobody would pretend that telling the truth is easy for Don Flow, or for that matter any other Christian out in the world. Flow sells Chevrolets, Saturns, and Hondas, and his personal desire to tell the truth cannot stand in isolation. It rests, in part, on the integrity of these auto manufacturers and the hundreds of other people who form the chain of making, selling, and servicing Flow's cars. Moreover, Flow operates his car business in a highly competitive environment, a marketplace where his competitors may not be as clear-eyed and honest as he wants to be. In other words, every Christian out in the world, Don Flow among them, lives and moves in systems and structures not entirely of our own making. "We fight not just flesh and blood," says the Apostle Paul, "but powers and principalities." We don't have stars in our eyes. We know that standing out there in the marketplace and promising to tell the truth, cross our hearts and hope to die, does not suddenly make language trustworthy and ethics clean. But truth-telling is a place to start.

God gave words to human beings as a treasure. God gave us words to tell the truth to each other, to build relationships of trust, to express love and belonging, to sing with joy, and to pray what is in our hearts. In a world that uses words as camouflage and as weapons, in a world that uses words as a kind of shell game to hide the truth, to have people who bravely tell the truth, the whole truth, and nothing but the truth is a radical, refreshing, and even disruptive event.

WISE TRUTH

To say that Christians are called to tell the truth out in the workaday world does not mean that it is a Christian thing to blurt out the un-varnished truth in any and all circumstances. Sometimes the plain facts are cold and hard. "You're dumb and lazy!" may be true, but those words are also cruel. A surgeon who strides into a patient's room and trumpets, "Well, the test results are in. You've only got a few weeks to live," may be telling the truth, but simple compassion would call for weighing the words more carefully.

Professor Peter Gomes, the distinguished preacher at Harvard University's Memorial Church, tells a story on himself about his experience with some not-so-edifying truth-telling. One Saturday morning, Gomes was working busily at the church office when the phone rang. He answered, and the voice on the other end asked, "Who is preaching there tomorrow morning?" Not wanting to put the caller on the spot by responding, "*I* am," Gomes simply described himself in the third person. "The preacher is the Minister in the Memorial Church and Plummer Professor of Christian Morals."

There was a pause at the other end of the line, and then the caller said, "Is that that short, fat, little, black man?" The annoyed Gomes curtly said, "Yes," and slammed down the phone.[6]

Reflecting later on this experience, Gomes wondered why he had gotten so upset. The caller, he decided, had not really intended to be insulting, inflammatory, or racist. In fact, the person on the other end of the line had actually said nothing that was not objectively true. The caller, however, not knowing that she was speaking to Gomes himself, had unintentionally done damage by puncturing his self-image. "Not that I think of myself as tall and blond or as a dead ringer for Denzel Washington," Gomes observed. "I usually think of myself, however, as more than the sum of my physical characteristics."[7]

So when is telling the whole truth a good thing, and when is it not? Over the generations, Christians have learned that the kind of truth we are most interested in, the kind of truth we are most called to tell, is measured not only by what it is but also by what it does. In Christian terms, truth is more like a verb than a noun. It causes things to happen. Christians, then, are not just concerned to gets the facts straight and to put bald truths on the table. They are alert to timing, effects, and relationships.

If someone had come up to me when I was in high school and trying to learn how to play the guitar and said, "Son, if you think you've got much talent for that, you are sadly mistaken," that would have been the truth, no doubt about it. But would it have been a good truth to tell me? On the one hand, it could have been just the dose of realism I needed, saving me from countless moments of public embarrassment and from years of self-deception and wasted time trying in vain to be the next Andres Segovia or Eric Clapton. On the other hand, it could have been severely deflating, causing me to turn in my picks and capos on the spot and depriving me of the joy, satisfaction, discipline, and self-awareness I was receiving from trying my best to master a musical instrument. After all, I would discover soon enough (in fact, I already had a pretty good inkling) that appearing at Carnegie Hall or playing lead in the Allman Brothers Band was not in my future. Christians don't just say things because they believe them to be true. God's truth is more complex than mere factuality. Words do things, words cause things to happen, words have consequences, and Christians take those consequences into account in speaking the truth.

In one of his essays, Walker Percy imagines a collection of top scientists, philosophers, and artists gathered for a big convention in Aspen, Colorado. They have come to read learned papers to each other and to take account of the most recent discoveries, theories, claims, and formulas in the various fields of knowledge. What would happen, Percy wonders, if in the middle of this convention, a fire broke out in the convention hall and a man rushed to the podium to say, "Come! I know the way out!" What would happen is that the hearers would immediately recognize that they had just heard a very different kind of speech. "The conferees will be able to distinguish at once," Percy says, "the difference between this sentence and all the other sentences which have been uttered from the podium."[8]

What makes the statement "Come! I know the way out!" different from, say, a statement about the chemical formula of a certain hydrocarbon? In the first place, "Come! I know the way out!" is a life-or-death truth claim that calls for action. The conferees cannot mull this statement over or record it for later testing in the lab. They have to get out of their seats and move. It calls for change and a response. Second, "Come! I know the way out!" is a statement that is received more in trust than on evidence. This implies that the trustworthiness of the man who made the statement is of utmost importance. Percy writes:

> If the newsbearer had announced, not that he knew the way out but that world peace had been achieved, they would hardly heed him. If he commanded them to flap their arms and fly out through the skylight, they would hardly heed him. If he spoke like a fool with all manner of ranting and raving, they would hardly heed him. If they knew him to be a liar, they would hardly heed him. But if he spoke with authority, in perfect sobriety, and with every outward sign of good faith and regard for them, saying that he knew the way out and they only had to follow him, they would heed him. They would heed him with all dispatch.[9]

In other words, what makes a truth like "Come! I know the way out!" different from other truths involves a combination of the veracity of what is said, the trustworthiness of the person who says it, and the life-giving effects for those who hear and heed it. This blend of person, message, and impact is the kind of truth Christians are called to tell. They want what they say to be true, but they also want to speak it in a trustworthy manner, and they want to speak a truth that matters to others, in fact, matters in a life-or-death way.

How can we know when we are speaking that kind of truth? What standards or measures can we apply? The key to truthful Christian speech lies not in some technique or method but in what we understand to be the basic values of our faith. It is a staple of old *New Yorker* cartoons and classic jokes for someone to ask some authority figure, say, a person at the library information desk or a department store Santa, "What is the meaning of life?" as if that person would know, as if someone would be able to put life's meaning into a one-sentence answer. But no one was joking when one day, an attorney asked Jesus a Jewish version of that very question: "Which commandment, out of all the commandments in the law, is the greatest one?" In other words, the lawyer wanted to know, "What is the key to this whole business of life? What is the central meaning of life?"

Jesus responded by naming not one but two commandments. The first, and greatest, he said, is "You shall love the Lord your God with all your heart, and with all your soul, and with all your mind." Then Jesus added a second commandment, which he said was like the first: "You shall love your neighbor as yourself." Everything else that matters, everything else in the law, Jesus said, derives from these two commandments.

To love God and to love one's neighbor. This is the essential message of our faith, these are the central goals in life, and everything can be organized around them. And these two goals form the standard for how Christians talk out in the world, the tests for Christian truth-telling. Christians seek to tell the truth not just to be accurate or to keep themselves safe from being caught in a lie. Christians tell the truth in order to increase the love of God and the love of neighbor. These are often hard tests to apply, but they are the yardsticks by which Christian testimony is measured.

Some comedians have made careers out of insulting people. In the full glare of stage lights and to people's faces, they say what most other people do in whispers and behind people's backs. By insulting people, these comedians demonstrate the dark side of words, the power of words to wound. They generate laughter by the shock value of words, by using words in exactly the opposite way that we sense they were intended to be used. Such words do not increase the love of God and neighbor. They avoid the love of God and tear down our regard for the neighbor. In short, they put people in their place.

Ironically, Christians, too, use words to put people in their place. But Christians have a different vision of "place." Christians believe that all people are created in God's image, that every person we meet, from the guy next to us on the subway to the woman stocking the shelves at the QuikChek to the teenager serving burgers at Wendy's, has been crowned by God "with glory and honor" (Psalm 8:5). This is the proper place of human beings, and we want to use words to put people in their place, their God-given place.

This conviction that people are crowned by God with glory and honor holds even for our enemies and even for people whose deeds dramatically deny the image of God in them. In August 1998, Sam Bowers was finally convicted, after four mistrials, of the vicious crime he had committed more than three decades before, the firebombing murder of Vernon Dahmer.

Before dawn on January 10, 1966, Bowers, who was then the Imperial Wizard of the White Knights of the Ku Klux Klan, and a number of his fellow Klansmen drove to Dahmer's house out in the country from Hattiesburg, Mississippi. While Dahmer and his family slept, the Klansmen doused their home with gasoline and set it on fire, destroying both the house and an adjoining grocery store. One of Dahmer's three children, a ten-year-old daughter, was injured in the fire. Dahmer himself lived for a few hours but died that afternoon. His crime? He had allowed black people to pay their poll taxes in his grocery store.

One of the individuals present in the courthouse for Bowers's 1998 trial was the Reverend Will Campbell. Campbell, a maverick Baptist preacher and former campus chaplain at the University of Mississippi well known for his outspoken views, had long been involved in the civil rights movement. When the Southern Christian Leadership Conference was established, Campbell was the only white person present. Later, he had bravely walked with the black students who first integrated Central High School in Little Rock, Arkansas, as they made their way through the angry mob in the street. In his days at Ole Miss, Campbell had known Vernon Dahmer and had worked closely with him on voting rights issues.[10]

Courtroom reporters were shocked, though, to see Campbell being embraced as an old friend not only by Ellie Dahmer, Vernon's widow, but also by the defendant, Klansman Sam Bowers. During recesses in the trial, Campbell was observed talking with equal warmth to both Ellie Dahmer and Sam Bowers. One of the newspaper reporters covering the trial asked Campbell how he could possibly be so friendly with both the victim and the vicious monster who had committed murder, the ever-salty Campbell replied, "Because I'm a Christian, G—dammit!"

Campbell recalled how, as a campus chaplain caught up in the civil rights movement, he had decided that as a Christian, he needed to spend time not only with his friends and people who shared his views but also with his enemies. As a result, he had met Sam Bowers and spent time with him. During one of their meetings, Campbell had been riding with Bowers in a car and Bowers had stopped by a local cemetery to pray at the gravesite of a friend. When he came back to the car, Campbell remembered, he was crying. "Animals don't cry," Campbell said. "Human beings cry at the foot of a friend's grave."[11]

Enemy or friend, stranger or companion, all people are seen by Christians as neighbors in Christ. When the waitress comes over to our table with the water pitcher and asks, "Is everything all right?" how should we respond? This is a simple, innocuous exchange; hundreds like it occur in a day. Who cares how we respond to the waitress? It may seem strange or overly fussy to think that we should concern ourselves with responding to her in a way that tells the truth and "increases the love of God and neighbor," but that is precisely what Christians are supposed to do. We are called to let our words be formed out of our faith, even if this just means that we look her in the eye and say, "Thank you," rather than staring at our soup and muttering, "Yeah." Speaking this kind of talk does not come easily. We have to think about it, learn it, and practice it. We need to go to school to acquire this skill, and the church is God's language school, teaching us to use words in ways that build up the love of God and neighbor.

Learning in Worship

When Christians are at worship—singing, praying, preaching, and passing the peace—they are not only praising God but also learning how to talk in the world. In Chapter Three, we saw that worship is a dress rehearsal for speaking faithfully in the rest of life. This is as true in the world of work as it is in personal relationships.

Imagine, for example, that a supervisor at an insurance company, who is a Christian, is to conduct an annual review of one of her employees. When the employee comes to her office for the evaluation, whom does she see? She obviously sees a coworker, a man with certain job responsibilities, perhaps a man who has performed well in some areas and who needs to improve in others. But because she has been in worship, she sees more than this. She has sung, "O come let us worship and bow down, let us kneel before the Lord our maker! For he is our God, and we are the people of his pasture" (Psalm 95:6–7). She has reached across the aisle and taken the hands of strangers, saying, "The peace of the Lord Jesus Christ be with you." She has heard the Scripture that tells how God said, "Let us make humankind in our image" (Genesis 1:26). She knows, then, that this is not just an employee of the company. This is a child of God, and she must speak in a way that honors this.

This does not mean, of course, that she will speak only sweetness and sugar. She will tell the truth, and this will inevitably involve pointing out weaknesses as well as strengths. But everything she says will be shaped by what her faith has taught her, and she knows that she does not have just a task; she has a ministry. This is not just a corporate exercise. Her task is not merely to evaluate this person but to honor him, to speak to him in a way that builds up the love of God and neighbor. She is the supervisor, and she must exercise the responsibility and power of that role. But she is also a Christian speaking to a fellow creature of God, and she will not lord herself over him, even if she must say difficult things to him.

According to the Gospel of Mark, a very affluent man once approached Jesus with a question about his soul. "Good teacher," he asked, "what must I do to inherit eternal life?"

"You know the commandments," Jesus replied.

"Indeed I do," said the man, "and I've kept every one of them since I was a little boy."

Now if we hit the fast-forward button on this story, we will discover that Jesus is about to say a hard thing to this man, something nobody would want to hear. Jesus is about to tell this man that his self-image is distorted and that his spiritual life is incomplete. Jesus is about to be utterly frank with this man and to level with him that he "lacks" in some essential aspect of human character. What is more, Jesus is about to lower the boom by telling this man that in order to recover his humanity and his relationship to God, he will need to do the one thing that will shake him to the core: sell every last thing he owns and give away the proceeds to the poor. This is where this story is going.

But don't hit the fast-forward button, because just before Mark tells us what Jesus says to the man, he names a detail we should not rush past. "Jesus, looking at him, loved him" (Mark 10:21). Before Jesus says what may be the toughest words this man has heard in his life, Jesus looks at the man and loves him. What Jesus says to him is not apart from this love or in spite of this love but an expression of this love.

Sometimes the hardest, most demanding words we speak to each other out in the world are born not of rage or offense but of love. Sometimes words that increase the love of God and neighbor are soft, encouraging, and warm, but sometimes they sound like, "One thing you lack . . ."

Sandra Herron is the vice-president at an Indiana bank. Several years ago, she was assigned responsibility for a new department at the bank, and she soon discovered she had inherited a problem employee—she calls her Mary. Mary showed up for work each day, but her contribution to the department was minimal. She was shy, withdrawn, and reluctant to offer any ideas. For whatever reasons, she had become an office drone, and her creativity was completely stifled.

It would have been easy for Sandra to ignore Mary or perhaps to arrange to have her transferred or even fired. But Sandra is a regular worshiper, and wearing the eyeglasses of Christian worship, she saw something else, something more, in Mary. Like Jesus with the rich man, she looked at Mary and loved her, and because she did, she talked to her in a different way.

"Now, Mary, I want you to reach down deep inside," Sandra said. "You are a very talented woman. If you had no time or financial constraints, what would you really like to do?"

After a moment of hesitation, Mary responded, suggesting an amazing new program for the department. Slightly stunned, Sandra praised her creativity and asked if she had any other ideas. Sandra could hardly believe her ears. Shy, taciturn Mary began to pour out imaginative innovations. "Soon the ideas were flowing like a waterfall!" Sandra said.

As her meeting with Mary came to a close, Sandra expressed her gratitude for all of Mary's wonderful insights. Mary looked at her with great emotion. "No one has ever asked for my ideas before," she said.

It is at moments like these, Sandra reflects, that "God sometimes gives me a glimpse of His vision: I call these 'kingdom break-throughs.'" Sandra adds, "Our personal behavior can serve as a testimony to what God in Christ has done for us and to the presence of God in our lives. As part of the new creation in Christ, we can offer the hope of change to others who may be struggling."[12]

When Christians like Sandra Herron go to worship, their ears are trained not only by words of blessing and love but also by the prophetic word that challenges the status quo. The Reverend William Sloane Coffin once remarked that one of the most unsettling acts a person could perform would be to stand up in the middle of a board of directors meeting of a large corporation and read the first verse of Psalm 24—"The earth is the Lord's and all that is in it." A company that heard and heeded that word would have to change the way it treats people, the marketplace, and the environment.

On a more basic level, Sandra Herron talks about how the prophetic word affected her at the bank. She notes that the banking industry, like many others, has a concept called "differentiated service strategies." This is a fancy euphemism for treating big profitable customers better than smaller ones. When big depositors show up at the bank, they might be assigned a personal banker or at least be channeled into shorter exclusive teller lines. These wealthier customers would be given special privileges, rates, and gifts.

In her church, however, Sandra had heard about the "priesthood of all believers," where all human beings stand equal before God. In worship, she had heard the biblical injunctions against showing partiality, such as James's word, "My brothers and sisters, do you with your acts of favoritism really believe in our glorious Lord, Jesus Christ. . . . You do well if you really fulfill the royal law according to the scripture, 'You shall love your neighbor as yourself.' But if you show partiality, you commit sin" (James 2:1, 8–9).

Her worship-shaped conscience caused her "to question this generally accepted practice." She asked potentially embarrassing questions, like "Is preferential treatment for special groups of customers legitimate? If so, when does such treatment become unfairly discriminatory [against] others?"

Such prophetic action on her job did not, in her case, get her into trouble with the bank, but it did throw her into a tangle of moral questions. "For the manager who prayerfully asks for the wisdom to raise the right issues," Sandra states, "the questions are endless. How do I respond to a colleague who says that there is no morality in pricing? How can I show special consideration for unique personal circumstances and still treat people fairly and impartially? Is shopping the competition an acceptable means of gathering market intelligence so that we might compete more aggressively?"[13] It is not a simple matter, Sandra has found, to speak out in the work place so that the love of God and the love of neighbor are increased. But she has been to worship, and she can strive to do nothing less.

The Lutheran Church of the Holy Spirit in Emmaus, Pennsylvania, is one of the many congregations that have recognized that Christians need support in deciding how to speak and act in their working lives. This congregation has formed the Monday Connection, a group that meets at a local restaurant the first Monday morning of each month. At each session, one of the members of the group presents a real-life, no-holds-barred case from work. For most of an hour, the case is discussed, sometimes even debated. Questions are asked, concerns are raised, Bible passages are read, and theological matters are cited. One of the founders of the group comments, "Whenever possible, the group tries to find ways in which the worship service of the previous day connected to the case study being presented. Was there something in the lessons, the sermon, the liturgy, or a hymn that related to the problem?" The goal of every discussion is the same: to help people discover what Christ would have them do or say in a specific situation in the workaday world.

THE OLD, OLD STORY

So Christians are out there in the workaday world using words the best they can to increase the love of God and neighbor. They speak affirming words, confronting words, forgiving and accepting words, words of prophetic challenge. But all of these words are finally not enough. If we are to tell the truth, the whole truth, and nothing but the truth, we must ultimately speak about God. For Christians, affirmation, loving confrontation, forgiveness, and prophetic challenge are not free-floating virtues. They are not good things done by good, civic-minded people. They are the way of God in the world. These are the things God is doing and saying, and we do them and say them because we want to shape our life according to the pattern of God's life. If we are aiming to increase the love of God and neighbor, then God is in the picture, God must somehow, somewhere, be named.

Remember what Dorothy Day said: "If I have achieved anything in my life, it is because I have not been embarrassed to talk about God." We pick our times, we are wise about our places, but we are finally not afraid to speak explicitly to others about our faith. In the business world, when a matter of great sensitivity and importance is to be discussed, it is often done over lunch. There is something about breaking bread together that sets the right context for sensitive conversation.

So let's go to lunch.

Chapter 6

CONVERSATION OVER LUNCH

"Got time to grab a quick bite to eat?"

Invitations like this one come from many directions. Somebody we work with pokes his head in our office doorway just before noon, a friend calls on the phone, or a neighbor steps across the driveway as we are getting into our car to say, "Any chance you're free for lunch today?" Sometimes there is little substance involved, just a desire to have some companionship and to avoid the loneliness of soup and a sandwich alone. But many times an invitation to lunch is an invitation to talk, to talk about stuff that matters. Get an invitation to breakfast, and that usually means business. Get an invitation to dinner, and that is sometimes formal or perhaps even romantic. But an impromptu invitation to lunch is for honest, let-your-hair-down talk, for sharing life, for turning off the computer, putting work aside, and talking.

MISTER ROGERS AND BEAUTIFUL FEET

I want to employ the idea of lunch conversation as a metaphor for those times when Christians are given the opportunity, or maybe even put on the spot, to talk about our faith. In Chapter Five, we explored how Christians talk when they go out into the workaday world, and the emphasis fell on talking *faithfully*. Faithful talk is telling the truth with the aim of increasing the love of God and neighbor, and this, as we saw, does not always involve explicitly religious talk. But now we want to think about those occasions that *do* involve explicitly religious talk, those "lunchtime conversations" in which talking faithfully means talking with others about faith, our faith, the other person's faith, the Christian faith.

When Fred Rogers of children's television fame died in early 2003, for several weeks afterward the news was filled with stories and remembrances of this kind and gentle man. One reporter remembered the day that Fred Rogers had been invited to address the prestigious National Press Club in Washington. The National Press Club is accustomed to hearing speeches from diplomats, top administration officials, and key opinion makers on the top issues of the day, and some members of the press had privately joked that with "Mister Rogers" on the podium, they were probably in for a "light lunch."

However, according to the reporter, when Fred Rogers stood up to speak, he said that he knew the room was filled with many of the best reporters in the nation, men and women who had achieved much. Rogers then took out a pocket watch and announced that he was going to keep two minutes of silence, and he invited everybody in the room to remember people in their past—parents, teachers, coaches, friends, and others—who had made it possible for them to accomplish so much. And then Mister Rogers stood there, looking at his watch and saying nothing. The room grew quiet as the seconds ticked away, but the reporter said that before Fred Rogers tucked away his watch, one could hear all around the room people sniffling as they were moved by the memories of those who had made sacrifices on their behalf and who had given them many gifts.

Likewise, if those of us who find meaning and comfort in the Christian faith were to take two minutes to reflect on how our faith came to be, few of us would say that we got it from a book, and none of us would say we thought it up on our own. Quickly or gradually, we would begin to remember the people who spoke to us about God. "Faith," the Apostle Paul once observed, "comes from what is heard" (Romans 10:17), and that is true about our faith, too. We heard and we believed; slowly or suddenly, in a moment of stillness or in a thunderstorm of passion, we believed. The faith we have, whether large or small, whether born of struggle or comfort, whether richly textured or barely patched together, whether grasped firmly or held onto by our fingernails, is a part of our lives because somebody along the way had the courage and the conviction to talk to us about God and about Jesus Christ.

I grew up in the American South of the 1950s, in what Flannery O'Conner once called the "Christ-haunted landscape." Southern society in those days was full of "God talk" and "Jesus saves talk," and my parents, both southerners, talked about God and Jesus, too. But they talked about their faith in ways that were both like the religious talk of other people and, at the same time, quite different. Compared to some other adults I knew, my parents seemed to have a surer sense that God is, indeed, a God of love. They had a strong understanding of Providence, God's loving care, which made them both humble and confident. They had a sense of humor and were alert to the ironic aspects of life and faith. They taught me the song that goes "Jesus loves the little children, all the children of the world. Red and yellow, black and white, they are precious in his sight," and they made it clear in the way they treated other people that they believed it.

My parents did not wear their religion on their sleeves; they wove it into the fabric of their everyday garments. They told me the stories of Jesus, they read to me from the Bible, and they prayed with me, but none of this jutted out from the rest of life's terrain. God talk was all bound up with homework talk, cut-the-grass talk, Cub Scout talk, and supper table talk. They probably didn't know it, but they were good lay theologians, theologians of the reality of God in the ordinary events of life, teaching me that the gifts of everyday life are the means of grace.

They weren't the only ones, though, who talked to me about faith. Among others were a childhood friend, a college roommate, a beloved professor, and a string of long-suffering Sunday school teachers. I sometimes wonder now if those kindly folk who taught me in Sunday school were second-guessing themselves all the time. The kids my age, as we progressed from childish cutups to flirtatious teenagers, could hardly have been very responsive, pious, or satisfying students.

One of our teachers, a former standout high school baseball player, so despaired of holding our attention that he punctuated a lesson on Moses and the burning bush with instructions on how to throw a curve ball. But they did it. They stood up there in front of often distracted children and talked about God. They dragged their weekday-weary bodies, their sometimes halting knowledge of the Bible, their own struggles with doubt, and their clearly evident humanity into spare Sunday school classrooms and dared to talk to other people's children as best they could about the Christian faith.

I look back now and realize how much what they did mattered, how much what they said continues to nourish what I believe and what I do with my life. Some people might point out that these people were not close to being Bible scholars—some of them had not even graduated from high school—and scoff at their lack of knowledge and their capacity for misinformation. Some others might sniff at their primitive pedagogy—their crinkled lesson books, their almost comical attempts to make cutout paper sheep stick to flannel boards, and their often futile struggles to instruct restless nine-year-olds—and call it a waste of time. I don't. I call it courage. I call it love. I call it faithful testimony.

Perhaps the same is true for you as well. We all have different experiences—yours is surely not the same as mine—but for all of us, whatever faith we have is there because somebody overcame the reluctance and took the time to speak to us about God. Somebody walked into a Sunday school class or climbed into a pulpit or dropped by your dorm room or sat with you beside the lake at camp or held on to you during a really bad time in your life and talked, maybe stammeringly, but talked nevertheless, to you about God. The Old Testament scholar James Sanders dedicated one of his books to some of the people who talked to him honestly about God and the Christian faith. The book, *God Has a Story, Too,* is dedicated to "Sisters Agnes and Iris and my sister, Nell, women who told me the tomb was empty, and Ruth and Joe Brown Love, who told me my head need not be."[1]

As we saw in Chapter One, the Bible contains a strange phrase to describe what it means that people come to us and speak about the faith: "How beautiful are the feet of those who bring good news" (Romans 10:15). The Bible says that people who bring good news, people who talk to other people about God, have beautiful feet, because our feet are what get us from here to there. The real good news, the kind of talk about God that matters in life, the kind of talk about God that is honest and freeing, cannot be shouted over the airwaves, plastered on a billboard, or mused about in the abstract. Somebody has to pick up his or her feet and go from here to there, from where he or she is to where we are, look us in the eye, and speak. No wonder, then, that on the very first Easter, when the women had gone to the cemetery to see the place of burial; no wonder then, that when the risen Christ met them on the path full of life over death and love over hate; no wonder, then, when he spoke to them and said, "Greetings!" his voice full of the grace and peace of God; no wonder, then, that they "took hold of his feet" (Matthew 28:9).

Michael Frost, in his book *Seeing God in the Ordinary: A Theology of the Everyday,* tells about a church where an unusual event occurred at the Christmas Eve service one year. A woman in the congregation had been asked to sing a solo, and she chose for the occasion, somewhat improbably, Bette Midler's pop hit "From a Distance." After each verse, the soloist sang the chorus, which states, "From a distance God is watching us, watching us from a distance." The basic idea of the song is that while the world may be a pretty messed-up place, if you move back far enough and take a God's-eye view, it looks better. After several rounds of this chorus, a woman in the front row had had all she could take. She suddenly jumped up and began singing, to the same tune, "God came near to us, God came near to us, God came near to us, at Christmas!"[2] Our faith rests on the truth that God came close in Jesus and spoke to us. The passing on of faith depends on people who in Jesus' name come close and speak to others.

Now to be sure, not all God talk is good talk, and not all of our memories about how people spoke to us of God are happy ones. Sometimes people who come close do not good but harm, wittingly or unwittingly. Most of us can remember people who lied to us about God, spoke idolatrously to us about a punitive God, talked to us about God in self-serving ways, or gave a testimony that ended up taking from us more than it gave. Some people spend years trying to overcome the bad messages delivered to them in the name of the faith, which makes it all the more urgent to learn how to speak of God so that the love of God and neighbor (even the "neighbor" who is yourself) is built up and not torn down.

CONVERSION OR CONVERSATION?

Recently I was driving across town at rush hour and scanning on the radio for a traffic report when the dial happened to pause on a Christian talk radio station. The talk show host was taking telephone calls from listeners that day, and a woman named Barbara had called in. Barbara had problems; Barbara had a lot of problems. She had problems with her boss at work. She complained about trouble in her marriage. She was at odds with her teenaged children. She said she had occasional bouts of depression.

As she unfolded her litany of troubles and woes, suddenly the talk show host interrupted her. "Barbara," he said, "I want to ask you something. Are you a believer? You know, you're never going to solve any of these problems unless you're a believer. Are you a believer?"

"I don't know," said Barbara hesitantly.

"Now, Barbara," said the host, "either you are a believer or you aren't. If you're a believer, you know it. You know it in your heart. Barbara, tell me, are you a believer?"

"I'd like to be," Barbara replied. "I guess I'm just more agnostic at this point in my life."

The talk show host reacted quickly to that. "Now Barbara, there's a book I've written that I want to send to you. In this book, I *prove* that Jesus was who he said he was and that he was raised from the dead. Now, if I send you this book and you read it, will you become a believer?"

"I don't know," she said. "I've had a lot of trouble from preachers."

"We're not talking about preachers," the host said. "We're talking about *proof!* I've got proof, irrefutable proof, that Jesus was who he said he was and was raised from the dead. Now, if I send this book to you, will you become a believer?"

Barbara was frustrated. "I don't think you're listening to me," she said. "I'm having trouble trusting at this point in my life."

"Barbara," he said, "we're not talking about trust. We're talking about *truth*. I have unassailable proof. Now, if I send it to you, will you become a believer?"

"I guess so," Barbara said. "Yeah, I'll become a believer."

Now, I know this may sound strange, but I'm a little sorry that Barbara threw in the towel so quickly. Please don't misunderstand. I, too, would like for Barbara to believe the gospel, and I, too, would like for her to find some help for her troubles in the Christian faith. But I also know that this talk show host stepped way out of bounds. He got it all wrong, and the main thing he got it all wrong about is words. He got it completely and tragically wrong about words.

First, he got it wrong about words and evidence, truth and trust. He wasn't telling the truth when he said he had irrefutable proof of the Resurrection. The fact is, there isn't any. There is no logical, scientific proof of the Resurrection. We don't have a videotape of Jesus vacating the tomb. We have no seismograph of the Easter earthquake. The fact is, all we have are words. All we have is testimony. The women who were at the tomb came back and told the story. The disciples told the story. From generation to generation, people have passed the stories of Jesus down to their children and to their friends and even to strangers, and some of these children, friends, and strangers have believed what they said and told the stories themselves.

This does not mean that we have only empty words or that we have only a likely story. What it means is that we don't first get some airtight scientific proof, some historically irrefutable evidence, and then base what we believe on that. What we have first is words. What we have first is the telling of the stories of Jesus and the gathering around them in faith. And when two or three are gathered around in faith and their eyes are wide open to God, the risen Christ comes to them and they know that what they have believed is not in vain.

The second way this talk show host got it wrong about words is that he misunderstood the character of Christian testimony. Christian

115

testimony is about telling the truth the best we can, telling the truth in such a way that other people come more fully alive, telling the truth so that both we and the people we talk to grow in the love of God and neighbor. The radio host, however, was trying to use words to talk Barbara into something—to coerce her, really—and it was fairly clear that this was more for his benefit than for Barbara's. He would deny this, of course, almost certainly arguing that he was only trying to save Barbara's soul, a most urgent task. But the truth is that he didn't know Barbara, didn't take the time to know her, was in fact impatient with her telling of her story. Barbara was not a fully real-ized person to him but an object. She was not really a "soul" in any Christian sense but a potential statistic. What he said to her was a sales pitch, not testimony. He was not interested in having a conversation, only in tallying a conversion. In Christian testimony, the end doesn't justify the means. The means and the end are the same: the truth, the whole truth, and nothing but the truth.

Before I come down too hard on this talk show host, though, perhaps I should examine the beam in my own eye. Probably the deepest reason this fellow was trying to get Barbara to believe was not that he wanted to carve a notch in the handle of his evangelistic six-shooter but rather that down in the hidden recesses of his life, his own faith is pretty fragile, and if he could get somebody like Barbara to agree that he was right about Jesus and the Resurrection, it would buttress his shaky conviction. Here I must join him in a *mea culpa*. Trying to persuade other people to believe what we believe, whether it's politics, parenting, or religion, is a classic device to shore up our own uncertainty. I have done this; probably most of us have. When other people doubt what we hold to be true, when they are skeptical about what we hold to be essential, when they find incredible our deepest credibilities, it is hard not to take this as a personal threat to our belief structure. When we ourselves are plagued with doubts, one tactic is to turn that energy outward and to fortify ourselves by seek-ing to persuade others.

The problem arises because, even though we might like to think of ourselves as rugged individuals with truly independent thinking ("Even if the whole world should deny the truth, I alone will never forsake my belief in what is right"), the fact is that important beliefs and values, including our religious convictions, are mostly socially maintained. In order to hold onto our beliefs, we need other people who believe them, too. This is not a bad thing; it's just a fact.

For example, suppose that for whatever reason, you happen to believe in the existence of elves. If you live in a village where everybody believes in elves and where the latest sightings are joyfully reported, your belief will probably remain undisturbed. But if you move to, say, Chicago, you may be in for trouble. If you talk about elves on the subway, you may find people edging away, eyeing you carefully to make sure you are not armed. If you openly talk about elves at work, you will probably find yourself stalled in your career or, worse, fired. If you talk about elves to your neighbors, people will warn their children not to go near your home. In short, you will find precious little support for your beliefs out there in the society of Chicago—in the neighborhood, at the university, in the library, at the office, or on the street. The result is that inevitably, you will be thrown into self-doubt. You, too, will wonder whether this whole elf thing was the product of a bad psyche or poor digestion. Only an extraordinarily resilient personality—or a psychotic—could persist forever in a belief that almost no one else shares. Stay in the city long enough, and your choices will boil down to two: either give up your belief in elves, or found a small group of the elf-faithful that will hold meetings in a bar near Wrigley Field on Thursday nights.

The point, of course, is not to equate Christian faith with belief in elves. The point is that almost any system of belief depends on a social structure to maintain it. Few of us who are Christians would be able to sustain our faith very long without the faithful Christian community around us. This has become even clearer to us now as the old social supports for Christianity break down in our society. If absolutely nobody else in the world believed in the Resurrection of Jesus Christ, if I were the only one, I would probably eventually crumple under the weight of others' disbelief.

Here, then, is the balancing act for Christian testimony. Yes, to hold on to our faith, we need each other. Yes, to stay faithful to God in Christ, I need you and you need me. If the people around us begin to have doubts about the faith, it won't be long before most of the rest of us have those doubts ourselves. But as we hold hands and support each other in our faith, the God who comes to us is the one who promises to provide such a community of faith, to build it up, and to sustain it. We learned about that in the Garden of Eden. It is not good for humanity to be alone, and God does not leave us alone—not in our need for intimacy, not in our hunger for companionship, and not in our faith. "I will build my church, and the gates of Hades will not prevail against it" (Matthew 16:18). This is what Jesus told us, and we trust him. We do not need to be anxious, then, that we will be left alone, and because we do not need to be anxious, we do not need to coerce people into believing as we do.

The more narrow and fearful our faith, the more we will need other people to toe the line and to believe exactly what we believe. Any deviation from our orthodoxy constitutes a threat, a threat to us and to our ability to hold on to our tightly wound system of belief. How we speak to other people about God will inevitably be stained with this anxiety and will tend to take the form of manipulation. The more confident, joyful, and trusting our faith is, the less we will need others to validate our every jot and tittle. The more we will know that our testimony is ultimately about God's goodness and not about our anxious need, is ultimately given as a gift to others and not as a self-serving attempt to put sandbags in the leaking levee of our own faith.

No Strings Attached

When we talk to other people about our faith, a basic goal, though an admittedly difficult one to achieve, is to say what we say as a gift, with no strings attached. Much talking in our culture is crassly self-seeking. The speaker wants something from the listener—a vote, a sale, a promotion, a contribution, a little sex, whatever—and is using words to get it.

Even when the motive is not so crass, much of our talk still wants something in return. When we say, "I love you," we sometimes say this mainly to stimulate the echo, "I love you, too." When we read a poem or sing a song or make a speech or preach a sermon, we are secretly hoping that people will think we did a good job and think well of us. When we offer a word of praise or encouragement, or even when we make a statement humbly asking that someone else be given a privilege instead of ourselves, is there not still the subtle motive of wishing to be thought a kind, humble, self-sacrificing person?

We can never be completely free of these secret longings for affirmation and reciprocation, but we can be self-aware and self-critical of them. When we talk to other people about God, insofar as it is in our power, we should give what we say as a gift that expects nothing in return. When we talk about God, we do so because we believe that what we are saying is true and that it will ultimately be a needed and welcome truth for the person who hears it. This means having the confidence and trust to say what we can say and to leave the results to God and the other person. This means letting go of any idea that what we say is valid only if the other person is persuaded by it, praises us for being so faithful, or thinks well of us for saying it.[3]

Late one cold winter's afternoon, my wife and I stood on the Maryland shore of the Chesapeake Bay, looking westward and watching the sun go down. Sunsets on the bay can be breathtakingly beautiful, but this particular sunset was, quite honestly, nothing to write home about. It was nice, but not anything like some of the color-drenched splendors of light we had seen before. I would have rated it, say, 4 on a scale of 10.

As the sun finally slipped completely beneath the gray waters of the bay, I turned around to watch our beagle lazily sniffing around in the marsh grass behind us, my eye following his meandering in and out of the reeds. I jammed my hands into my jacket pockets against the cold, and I was about to walk back to the house when I became aware that my wife was tugging on my sleeve and trying to get my attention. "Look, look!" she had been saying for I knew not how long. I turned around to the surprise that in the short moment I had looked away, the western sky had been transformed. This sunset had saved its best for last, had waited for the sun to disappear before releasing its magic. Like the glowing coals of a dying fire whose flames have already vanished, the sunless sky had begun to burn with an array of

Conversation over Lunch

vibrant oranges and yellows. This latecomer of a sunset was one of the most stunning we had yet seen. One of us wished aloud for a camera and then immediately whispered that no camera on earth could hold this luminous sight.

What did I learn from this? I suppose you could say I learned that it is a stupid thing to rate sunsets on a scale of 1 to 10, and maybe I also learned that Yogi Berra was right: "It ain't over till it's over." But mostly I learned something about gift-giving speech. When my wife urged me, "Look, look!" this was for my sake, not hers. She could see the sunset; I couldn't, and she did not want me to miss it. She was not seeking some form of validation, some sentimental cooing sound, "Oh baby, you are such a good judge of sunsets." She sought nothing for herself. She was just looking at this absolutely luscious and bodacious display of the glory of God, and I was facing in the wrong direction. So she wrapped it up in words and gave it to me as a gift.

So it is with testimony. We see the hand of God at work in life, and we don't want other people to miss it. Our main concern is not to scold people for facing in the wrong direction or to try to impress them with our piety. We don't want anything from them in return. We just want to give them the same gift that has been given to us over and over. When life is ablaze with the glory of God, what else can we do but say, "Look, look!"

SETTING THE TABLE FOR LUNCH

If talking about God is an act of true gift giving, then it takes place in the environment of hospitality. In the Christian sense, hospitality means more than just being friendly. It is more like a host setting the table for guests, preparing a place where people can find welcome, be nourished, and freely express themselves. Hospitality is a gift given to others, the gift of freedom. The Catholic theologian Henri Nouwen says that hospitality is

the creation of a free space where the stranger can enter and become a friend instead of an enemy. Hospitality is not to change people, but to offer them space where change can take place. It is not to bring men and women over to our side, but to offer freedom not disturbed by dividing lines. It is not to lead our neighbor into a corner where there are no alternatives left, but to open a wide spectrum of options for choice and commitment. It is not an educated intimidation with good books, good stories and good works, but the liberation of fearful hearts so that words can find roots and bear simple fruit.[4]

Nouwen displayed some of the very hospitality he describes in an encounter he had with the author Dan Wakefield. Wakefield, after years of "seeking salvation through drugs, alcohol, and promiscuity," as he puts it, began in the early 1980s to experience a spiritual awakening. He says that he developed what can be "best described as a 'thirst' for spiritual understanding and contact: to put it bluntly, I guess, for *God*."[5]

Wakefield, as is the case with many pilgrims, found the journey to God exhilarating but also filled with perils, self-doubts, and unexpected setbacks. He said he sometimes felt like an unfortunate passenger in an old prop airplane, the kind that you see in the 1930s adventure movies, "caught in a thunderstorm, bobbing through the night sky over jagged mountains without a compass."[6] Very tentatively, Wakefield had started attending church services, and when he told his minister about his spiritual struggles, the minister recommended that he read the book *Reaching Out* by Henri Nouwen. Wakefield found in Nouwen's prose welcome guidance for his journey, and so he read other books by Nouwen, including *A Cry for Mercy: Prayers from the Genesee,* in which Nouwen shared that he, too, sometimes experienced anguish and confusion in his own spiritual quest.

Wakefield wanted to meet Nouwen personally, and he was thrilled when Nouwen agreed to have lunch with him. As they ate together, Wakefield expressed his appreciation and admiration for Nouwen and his writing but confessed that Nouwen's confession in *A Cry for Mercy* about his own struggles had actually discouraged him. If someone as spiritually mature as Nouwen still wrestled with his doubts and anguished over his faith, what hope, Wakefield wondered, could there be for a mere beginner like himself? In reply, Nouwen could have patted Wakefield on the hand and said, somewhat condescendingly, "There, there, my son, you'll get stronger by and by," or he could have given him a prayer exercise to do or the title of another book to read, like a doctor's prescription. Instead he simply put down his fork and told Wakefield that contrary to popular opinion, "Christianity is not for getting your life together."[7]

That may seem like a strange form of witness, a peculiar testimony, to say only "Christianity is not for getting your life together." But what Nouwen was doing was following his own insight: "Hospitality is not to change people but to offer them space where change can take place." His words to Wakefield were an attempt to create just such a hospitable space, and sure enough, several years later, when some severe life jolts sent Wakefield spiraling back to seek relief in drugs, wisdom of what Nouwen said allowed the experience to be not a total defeat but a season of growth. Throughout the episode, Wakefield continued to cling to his faith until "the storm broke, like a fever." "I was grateful," Wakefield said, "but I also knew such storms would come again, perhaps more violently. I learned that belief in God does not depend on how well things are going, that faith and prayer and good works do not necessarily have any correlation to earthly reward or even tranquility, no matter how much we wish they would and think they should."[8]

TABLE TALK

When the time has come to talk about our faith, what do we say? When a friend facing some trouble wonders if we think praying is a helpful thing to do, or the guy next to us on a plane points to a news article about some church scandal and mutters how he just cannot understand why people waste their time with such a bunch of hypocrites, or when one of our children asks, "Mommy, can you see God?" the time has come to speak, to give our testimony. Most of us are, at best, amateurs at this sort of thing, and we can easily feel that knowing so little, we should keep our mouths shut and say nothing.

The biblical story often called "the loaves and the fishes" (John 6:1–14) may be helpful as we think about this tendency to be shy in what we say. In this story, a huge crowd of people had gathered around Jesus, and the problem came up of how to feed such a large number of people. Andrew, one of the disciples, pointed out, probably rather sheepishly, that a boy was there who had five loaves of bread and a couple of fish, hardly enough to feed a multitude. However, Jesus took the loaves and the fish, in other words took what they had, gave thanks for it in a prayer, and gave it to the crowd. Amazingly, the little bit of food had been transformed into a feast. Not only was there enough to satisfy the hunger of the crowd, but it took a dozen baskets to hold the leftovers.

This is a bad news–good news kind of story, or maybe we should say a bad-news-that-turns-out-to-be-good-news story. On the "bad news" side, the story is quite frank that none of us has what it takes to feed other people, and this goes for testimony, too. If the disciples had been left to their own devices, that crowd would have left fighting over a few scraps of food. Five loaves and two fish would hardly have cut it. Just so, if testimony depended on our deep wisdom and knowledge of God, we and those who hear us would be on a starvation diet. When the question comes up "Why do bad things happen to good people?" or "How do we know what God's will is?" or "Does God really answer prayer?" who among us is wise enough to fully satisfy those concerns? We have only fragments and pieces—loaves and fishes—to offer, and by themselves, they are not enough.

And yet they are enough. The "good news" part of the story is that God takes what we offer, takes our fragments and pieces and bits of experience and knowledge, and makes them sufficient, even abundant. Down through the years, very few Christians have been as courageous as Luther, as wise as Augustine, or as saintly as Mother Teresa, but the faith has been spread by the honest talk of ordinary Christians saying as best we can what we know and believe. Loaves and fishes? Yes, but also a banquet of testimony.

LOAVES AND FISHES

What fragments of testimony do we bring? If we are not a seminary theologian or a biblical scholar, what witness do we have to offer? First, every Christian can speak honestly about his or her own religious experience. The great leader of the church in India, D. T. Niles, once described sharing the faith as "one beggar telling another beggar where to find food." The Catholic scholar Hans Kung wrote a massive book called *On Being a Christian,* and in the introduction claimed that he had written it "not because the author thinks that he is a good Christian, but because he thinks that being a Christian is a particularly good thing."[9] Every Christian can speak with that kind of humility and honesty, saying in effect, "Here is what I have experienced. I am not claiming that it is perfect or enough or even very good, but I believe that it has led me to a very good thing."

We also know that our little fragments and episodes are part of a larger story, a holy story. We know this because we have been in worship, and one of the things that worship does is unfold the great sweeping story of God's love affair with the world, from creation to the end of time, and then point the finger at every last one of us and announce, "You're in this story. This is your story, too." When we were baptized, we crossed the Red Sea with Moses and the Israelites, and we plunged down into the Jordan River with Jesus. Every Sunday, we walk right into God's house, dragging along with us the anxieties and joys of life—like worrying about our kids and drugs or trying to figure out just which way to turn next in our job or feeling so grateful for that new grandchild we spent the week bouncing on our knee—and we place the whole confusing episodic tangle of it in the offering plate and say, "God, make sense of this." And God takes the little half-baked subplots that make up our lives, the little loaves and fishes, and does a little rewriting and, behold, they have become part of the biggest, best, most hopeful drama of all. No matter how episodic our life may seem when we are living it day to day, worship lets us see that we are actually key actors in a grand and holy narrative, and if we are paying attention, we walk out of worship knowing that life is a sacred drama and ready to tell whoever will listen that we are all playing important roles, sacred roles.

This sense of the narrative wholeness of human life is a crucial dimension of testimony precisely because, apart from the insight of faith, life can seem permanently random, arbitrary, and meaningless. For example, many contemporary novels do not have a complete sense of plot, that is, they don't have clear beginnings, middles, and ends, and this is not merely a literary convention but an expression of the way life is experienced. One novelist, Renata Adler, said that she wrote her first novel "waiting for a plot to emerge," but in vain. "I used to think," she said, "that at some point you'd see your life as a long narrative swing, that at some point you could see the shape of things and all the different strands would come together. Now I don't. You can find a plot to a week or a couple of days, but not much more, not to a lifetime."[10]

Christians know what Adler is talking about. They know that the days whirl by and the unexpected happens. They know that plans are made to be changed and that life can seem like a jigsaw puzzle missing some of the pieces. If we are left on our own, Adler has it right. You can forge a plot for a couple of days but not for a lifetime. What have you got? Five loaves and two fish; that's about it. Not enough to feed a crowd, not enough to make a plot. But Christians also know a secret: we are not left on our own. As the psalmist put it, "Lord, you have been our dwelling place in all generations" (Psalm 90:1), and as Paul said, "Your life is hidden with Christ in God." A great story is being told, and we are part of it.

The playwright Thornton Wilder once imagined that life in God's care is like a beautiful tapestry. When viewed from the pattern side, the "correct" side, the tapestry has an intricate and magnificent design. The problem is that in our everyday lives, we cannot see the pattern. We live our lives on the reverse side of the tapestry, so what we see is only broken threads and knots. Only here and there, in worship and in moments of insight, do we glimpse what we will ultimately see in the full light, the great design of God's tapestry, the full plot of God's story.[11] Worship gives us a kind of "sneak preview" of

Conversation over Lunch

God's future. From the vantage point of worship, we can fast-forward to that time when we will see the full design of God, will see how the little moments and episodes of life have been fitting into a pattern hidden from our view. In her memoir *One Writer's Beginnings,* the famed short-story writer Eudora Welty said that writing about her life was like traveling on a train at night. "And suddenly a light is thrown back, as when your train makes a curve, showing that there has been a mountain of meaning rising behind you on the way you've come, is rising there still, proven now through retrospect."[12] Similarly, in worship we get a glimpse over the whole span of time and can see how the whole is shaped. C. S. Lewis once imagined that when we get to heaven, we will say to God, "So, it was *you* all along. Everyone I ever loved, it was you. Everything decent or fine that ever happened to me, everything that made me reach out and try to be better, it was you all along."[13]

Another novelist, John Updike, in describing the influence of the Christian faith on his own writing, pointed toward the relationship between worship and the sense of a sacred narrative. "Yes, I have been a churchgoer," he said, ". . . and the Christian faith has given me comfort in my life and, I would like to think, courage in my work. For it tells us that truth is holy, and truth-telling a noble and useful profession; that reality around us is created and worth celebrating; that men and women are radically imperfect and radically valuable."[14]

So we can say that life is a story told by God and we are part of it. Not only that, we can also honestly say that God has been with us at every tick of the clock, in every mood and moment of life. On Ash Wednesday several years ago, one of my friends, a hospital chaplain, left the hospital shortly before noon and attended a service at a nearby church. As a part of the worship, the minister inscribed on my friend's forehead a cross made of ashes mingled with oil. He returned to the hospital, ashes still in place, and began to visit the patients. One of the patients, a woman, noticed the ashes on his forehead and, thinking it was a smudge of dirt, grabbed a tissue, spit on it, and said, "Come here, hon, you've gotten into something."

My friend artfully avoided the tissue and said, "No, they are ashes. They're supposed to be there." She looked at him, puzzled. He began to talk to her about the meaning of Ash Wednesday, how the day meant that God was with us when we were weak and vulnerable, how we were but dust, ashes, and God was with us, taking us toward Easter even when life was broken, tragic, and sad.

The woman thought for a moment, and then she said, "I think I want some of that." My friend slowly reached to his forehead, borrowed some of the ashen smudge, and with his finger traced on her forehead the sign of the cross.[15]

Finally, every Christian can celebrate and talk about those experiences in life when God's presence has been palpable and real to us. Once I was with a church group in which people were asked to talk about times in their lives when God was close and real. One of the group was a young woman who was a dancer in a professional ballet company. When it came time for her to speak, it was clear that she was more comfortable as a dancer than as a speaker. She spoke hesitantly, haltingly.

She reminded the group that she was raised in that particular church. She described the sanctuary, including the baptismal font, and she said that she was baptized as an infant right in that very font. She did not remember this, of course, but she told us that her father was very proud of that moment and that when she was a little girl, he would often tell her of the Sunday that she was baptized. He would describe the baptismal dress that she wore, he would remember what hymns were sung and what the minister had said in the sermon, and he always ended the story by clapping his hands together and exclaiming, "Oh, sweetheart, the Holy Spirit was in the church that day!"

She then said that as a child, she would go to worship on Sunday with her parents and would wonder, "Where is the Holy Spirit in this church?" She would look at the brass organ pipes, at the rafters in the ceiling, and at the stained-glass windows, and she would wonder, "Is *that* where the Holy Spirit is in this church?"

Then she paused for a moment, and everybody in the room leaned forward to hear what she would say next. "As many of you know," she continued, "I lost both of my parents to cancer in the same week, a terrible week, last winter. During that awful week, on a dark Wednesday afternoon, I was driving home from visiting my parents in the hospital, and I was passing by the church. I felt an intense need to pray, and so I came into the church and sat in one of the back pews and began to pray. The church was dark, and in the shadows, I prayed and poured out my grief to God, and cried from the bottom of my heart. A member of the church," and here she named her, "was in the kitchen preparing a meal for a church meeting, and she saw me praying and knew what was happening in my life. She took off her apron, came and sat beside me in the pew, held my hand, and prayed with me. It was then," the young woman said, "that I knew where the Holy Spirit was in this church."

If we will think honestly and deeply about our lives, we all have experiences like that, moments when the presence of God is alive for us. These are our loaves and fishes, and if we will talk about them to others, spread them on the table of hospitality, God will make of them a great feast.

Chapter 7

THE SIX O'CLOCK NEWS

A cartoon that caught my eye showed a typical corner tavern with several business types huddled at the bar cradling cocktails. Every eye in the place is focused on the television over the bar, where a CNN-type newscaster is saying, "Jitters on Wall Street today over rumors that Alan Greenspan said, 'A rich man can as soon enter Heaven as a camel fit through the eye of a needle.'"[1]

It is funny, of course, to imagine the Federal Reserve chairman quoting Jesus on the dangers of wealth rather than talking about price indexes and market trends. At least some of the humor derives from the collision of worlds, the incongruity of having Jesus' words, which come from one context, spill out of the mouth of Alan Greenspan, who belongs to another context. We can no more imagine the Fed quoting Jesus than we can contemplate a preacher reading the stock ticker from the pulpit. It seems out of place, and when Alan Greenspan sounds like a prophet instead of pushing for a profit, you know it's a punch line.

Beneath the humor and good fun of the cartoon, however, lies a more basic question. Why would we think a saying of Jesus is out of place here? Do we really believe for a minute that Jesus' words are just "religious" words, which are fine for church and Bible study but have no place on Wall Street? In 1863, when President Lincoln established the holiday Americans call Thanksgiving, he showed no reluctance whatsoever to employ explicitly religious and biblical language. He called for "a day of thanksgiving and praise to our beneficent Father who dwelleth in the heavens." With the anguish of the Civil War on his heart, Lincoln spoke openly of public sin, encouraging the nation "with humble penitence for our national perverseness and disobedience" to commend to God's care the widows, orphans, and sufferers of the war, praying for Almighty God to "heal the wounds of the nation." In a century and a half, then, our society has moved from a time when a national leader could use serious theological language in a public proclamation to the point where the very idea is a punch line for a cartoon.

SILENCE ON THE PUBLIC SQUARE

Here is a strange paradox. On the one hand, most Christians today would be quite willing to say that Christianity involves every aspect of life. It makes claims on our time, our money, our work, our relationships, and our politics. On the other hand, however, many of these same Christians prefer to live out their faith in only very personal, very private ways. Despite the fact that we know better, many faithful Christians operate as if Christianity and Wall Street, Christianity and politics, or for that matter Christianity and public life generally are separate worlds best held at arm's length.

In his book *The Culture of Disbelief,* Stephen L. Carter argues that not only has religion been silenced in public discussion, but it is ignored and unwelcome. He notes, for example, that in 1983, when President Reagan gave a speech saying that all of the laws enacted since biblical times "have not improved on the Ten Commandments one bit," he was roundly criticized in the press for his reference to religion. Reagan, said one critic, was giving "short shrift to the secular laws and institutions that a president is charged with protecting." Likewise, Carter points out, when Hillary Clinton wore a necklace with a cross to some of the events connected to her husband's inauguration, one of the network commentators

130

TESTIMONY

raised the question of whether this display of religion was "appropriate," and when *Newsweek* ran a cover story on the topic of prayer, at least one letter to the editor angrily dismissed the article as a waste of space and called it "a theocratic text masquerading as a news article."[2]

There are good reasons why we get nervous about religion in the public square, of course. The relationship between church and state is a complex legal and social matter in our culture, and few Americans would want to contemplate a society controlled by religion, especially any *one* religion. When a Christian judge in Alabama put a stone monument inscribed with the Ten Commandments in the lobby of the county courthouse, even some very conservative Christians objected. This was not because they did not endorse the Ten Commandments—they did—but because they realized how dangerous it can be when any one religion gets to call the shots, even when that religion is their own.

But it is a sad consequence of the separation of church and state when religion (except the blandest and most civically acceptable variety) is banished from public life altogether and when Christian faith is silenced in public affairs. Yes, Christianity is about personal concerns and matters of the heart, but it is also about poverty and wealth, war and peace, justice in the courts, and protecting the weak. Early Christians did not worship in the catacombs because they liked the cool subterranean air. They worshiped there because the emperor recognized that Christianity had political implications and was a threat to the empire. Many of the great social movements of our own recent history, from abolition of slavery to women's suffrage to civil rights, have drawn inspiration from Christianity. Christianity is concerned with Sunday prayers, but because it prays on Sunday for God's will to be done, Christians are also concerned with what they see and hear when they turn on the six o'clock news. "In our sensible zeal to keep religion from dominating our politics," Stephen Carter says, "we have created a political and legal culture that presses the religiously faithful to be other than themselves, to act publicly . . . as though their faith does not matter to them."[3]

In the World but Not of It

We need to confess, though, that a powerful reason why Christians are often silent about faith in the public square is not from external pressure but from internal fear and reluctance. Most alert Christians recognize that the more we believe and trust in the gospel, the more we are aware that our faith is countercultural. The more our life is shaped after the pattern of Jesus Christ, the more we find ourselves in tension and conflict with the values of the world around us. Testimony can get us in trouble, because telling the truth is not always welcome, and it can be much more comfortable just to keep our faith in the privacy of our hearts.

The book of Acts tells how the early Christians gave their witness and testimony to the world. It begins very nicely. After Pentecost, the Christian community had "the goodwill of all the community" (Acts 2:47). But hardly one more chapter goes by before that goodwill has dissipated, society has realized that the gospel challenges the status quo, and the first Christian witnesses have been tossed into jail (Acts 4:3). "Evangelism," writes the biblical scholar Walter Brueggemann, "is no safe church activity that will sustain a conventional church, nor a routine enterprise that will support a societal status quo. Evangelism . . . is an activity of *transformed consciousness* that results in an altered perception of world, neighbor, and self, and an authorization to live differently in that world. The news that God has triumphed means . . . [bringing] more and more of life, personal and public, under the rule of this world-transforming, slave-liberating, covenant-making, justice-commanding God."[4]

The Harvard preacher Peter Gomes once got a taste of just how controversial a seemingly gentle gospel message can be. He gave a commencement address at a posh Manhattan private high school for girls. The students in this school were for the most part headed to the Ivy League or other elite schools and then on to careers of power and influence. Gomes preached what he thought was a lyrical sermon on Jesus' invitation to "consider the lilies of the field, how they grow; they toil not, neither do they spin, yet their heavenly father provides for them." Gomes emphasized what he considered to be Jesus' sound and comforting advice, "Therefore do not be anxious about tomorrow."

At the reception afterward, however, a father of one of the girls came up to Gomes "with fire in his eyes and ice in his voice." He told Gomes that what he said in his sermon about anxiety was complete nonsense. Gomes pointed out that it was Jesus, not he, who had actually said it, but the man would not be dissuaded. "It's still nonsense," he said. "It was anxiety that got my daughter into this school, it was anxiety that kept her here, it was anxiety that got her into Yale, it will be anxiety that will keep her there, and it will be anxiety that will get her a good job. You are selling nonsense."[5]

Sometimes Christian witness even seems insane by prevailing social standards. In 1968, a group of Christians led by a Catholic priest, Father Daniel Berrigan, protested the war in Vietnam by burning draft records taken from a draft board office in Catonsville, Maryland. They were arrested for this and tried in a case known as the Catonsville Nine. When Berrigan was questioned on the witness stand, his testimony was full of references to his theology and his faith, but the judge in the trial was puzzled by this and had difficulty understanding the connection between Berrigan's religion and his actions. When Berrigan was asked explicitly, "Was your action at Catonsville a way of carrying out your religious beliefs?" Berrigan answered clearly: "Of course it was. May I say if my religious belief is not accepted as a substantial part of my action, then the action is eviscerated of all meaning and I should be committed for insanity."[6]

Again, we can see the collision of Christian testimony and the larger culture in the case of Grace Thomas, a gentle Christian woman raised in the Southern Baptist Church. Not many people remember Grace Thomas today; indeed, I had almost forgotten about her myself until I chanced across her obituary in the morning paper some years ago and had my memory of her stirred. There was a time, though, when virtually everyone in the state of Georgia knew who she was.

Grace was the second of five children born to a Birmingham, Alabama, streetcar conductor and his wife. When she married in the late 1930s, she moved to Atlanta and took a clerking job in one of the state government offices. Through her work, she developed an interest in law and politics, and she enrolled in a local law school that offered night classes.

After years of part-time study, she finally completed law school, and her family wondered what she would do with her law degree. They were shocked when Grace announced that she had decided to enter the 1954 election race for governor of Georgia. There were nine candidates for governor that year—eight men and Grace—but there was really only one issue. In the famous case of *Brown* v. *Board of Education of Topeka* earlier that year, the U.S. Supreme Court had declared that racially "separate but equal" schools were unconstitutional and thus paved the way for the integration of the public schools. Eight of the gubernatorial candidates spoke out angrily against the court's decision. Only Grace said that she thought the decision was fair and just and ought to be welcomed by the citizenry. Her campaign slogan was "Say Grace at the Polls." Not many did; she came in dead last, and her family was relieved that she had gotten this out of her system.

But she had not. Eight years later, in 1962, she ran for governor again. By then, the civil rights movement was gaining momentum, and her message of racial harmony was hotly controversial. She received death threats, and her family traveled with her as she campaigned in order to provide protection and moral support. She finished last again on election day, but her campaign was a testimony to goodwill and racial tolerance.

One day, Grace made a campaign appearance in the small town of Louisville, Georgia. In those days, the centerpiece of the town square in Louisville was not a courthouse or a war memorial but an old slave market, a tragic and evil place where human beings had once been bought and sold. Grace chose the slave market as the site for her campaign speech, and as she stood on the very spot where slaves had been auctioned, a hostile crowd of storekeepers and farmers gathered to hear what she would say. "The old has passed away," she began, "and the new has come. This place," she said, gesturing to the market, "represents all about our past over which we must repent. A new day is here, a day when Georgians white and black can join hands to work together."

This was provocative talk in the Georgia of 1962, and the crowd stirred. "Are you a communist?" someone shouted at her.

Grace paused in midsentence. "No," she said softly. "I am not."

"Well, then," continued the heckler, "where'd you get those gall-durned ideas?"

Grace thought for a minute, and then she pointed to the steeple of a nearby church. "I got them over there," she said, "in Sunday school."

Because of her faith, Grace Thomas gave courageous testimony that day, but when lessons learned in Sunday school put us in harm's way out in the world, no wonder Christians are sometimes more than content to keep their faithful thoughts to themselves.

Proclaiming from the Housetops

Despite our inclination to keep our religion to ourselves, Christians know that we are called to a public expression of our faith, and this includes our speech, our spoken testimony, as well as our actions and good deeds. "What you hear whispered," Jesus told his followers, "proclaim from the housetops" (Matthew 10:27), or to put it another way, Jesus tell us that what we talk about quietly and privately in worship we should also talk about openly and publicly in our jobs, our politics, and our civic life. We take our cues, then, about what we say outside church from what is said inside church in worship.

Sometimes our testimony, like the opening words of a service of worship, serves as an announcement that "God is here!"—a verbal reminder that God is present and at work in the world. Lillian Daniel is a United Church of Christ minister and a thoughtful and grace-filled Christian who once found herself arrested on the steps of the Connecticut governor's office. What had happened was that poorly paid and poorly treated workers in state-run nursing homes had gone on strike, but the strike had failed. However, when the strikers returned, downtrodden, to work, they found themselves locked out of their jobs and replaced by temporary workers. So Lillian Daniel and several other clergy gathered with the workers on the governor's steps in protest. As they sat there, they all sang "Amazing Grace" as a sign of their faith and their hope and as a testimony to the compassionate presence of God.

The police were called, and some arrests were made, including Daniel. A pastor, a wife, and a mother, she experienced the shock of being rudely tossed into a paddy wagon and left all alone. "I had not expected," she said, "to be searched with rubber gloves, to have my things taken away, to lose the wallet snapshots of my grinning, toothless children, to be kept alone for such a long time." As she peered out of the paddy wagon through the small window, she could see the face of a police officer. She tells of their exchange:

"This stuff is pretty inhumane, isn't it?" he said.
 "I feel like an animal in a cage," I said.
 "And you're getting the royal treatment."
 "Thanks," I said.
 "If it makes you feel any better," he added, "I spent two nights in one of those things with a bunch of drunks, back in the military. You don't even want to know. It was disgusting."[7]

The two of them had now established some rapport, enough so that the policeman felt free enough to describe his own life struggles and his distaste for his job. Daniel continues:

"Why are you in this field, if you hate it so much?" I asked, perhaps wondering about my own future in my field.
 "Just fell into it I guess. After the military. So I retire in two years, and I'm young. But what I wanted to say to you was back there, when you guys were singing 'Amazing Grace,' in the capitol building. I liked that. I liked the way your voices sounded when you sang those songs. So I wanted to let you know."
 "Thanks again," I said.
 "You'll get out of here soon," he said.
 "You, too," I said.[8]

When the policeman told her that he liked her singing, he was almost surely talking about more than the sound of their voices. To

TESTIMONY

hear the witness of "Amazing Grace" in the midst of often bleak circumstances was a ray of hope for him. Thinking about this later, Daniel said, "If there's a way of life and of death, they flip quickly. The holy imagination can paint a picture of a new life where there are no bars and chains. His story about our singing, our practice of the faith, allowed me to imagine once again a world in which no one is locked in, or locked out."[9]

John Lewis, who is today a member of the U.S. House of Representatives, remembers the power of Christian testimony in his days in the civil rights movement. Lewis was an associate of Martin Luther King Jr. He marched with King at Selma, rode with the Freedom Riders on the bus trips, and was often the victim of police violence. Part of the power of those experiences, he says, was that they were not just silent protests but that they were accompanied by prayers, sermons, and spirituals. He says, "That's what made me feel when we were at the height of the civil rights movement—whether it was the march from Selma to Montgomery or going on the Freedom Rides—that we were involved in something like a Holy Crusade. It was an extension of my religious convictions, or my faith. We would sing a song or say a prayer and it was an affirmation that it was the right thing to do."[10]

If our testimony in the public square sometimes sounds like the opening words of worship, words that say in effect, "Sing to the Lord a new song, sing to the Lord all the earth," it also sometimes sounds like a call to confess our sins. Telling the truth is often telling the hard truth about failure, distortion, and human complicity in evil. Mary Munford is an Emmy Award–winning television newswriter who sees her job as an arena for Christian witness. Part of this witness is educational. As a newsperson, she has the ministry of providing accurate and reliable information to the public. But her testimony does not stop with information alone. She says that "in addition to 'speaking the truth' by providing useful information, journalists also have the opportunity to 'reveal the truth.' It is their responsibility to uncover information about corruption, mismanagement, and injustice." This uncovering of information about human wrongdoing is something that Christians practice every week in worship when we are called to confess our own sins and, in response to our confession, hear a word of forgiveness and a call to live an ethically responsible life. As Mary Munford puts it, "Over and again the Bible reveals a God who calls us both to do and to love justice."[11]

A monument at Auschwitz, one of the Nazi death camps, reads "O earth, cover not their blood." Sometimes a public Christian call to confession takes the form of recovering the public memory, of refusing to forget and cover up the blood of an evil that has been done. Whether it is the restless attempt to recover nearly forgotten slave narratives or relentless efforts to pry loose the truth about sexual abuse in the church, whenever Christians seek to uncover the truth, to bring a wrong from the shadows into the light, this refusal to forget is a testimony to the God who hears the cries of the downtrodden. As Rowan Williams, the archbishop of Canterbury, has said, "History does *not* ultimately lie in the hands of the slaughterer. The dead *can* be named; the past must be known. In that naming and knowing, God is to be met; and in God lies the possibility for us of a different world, a different apprehension of power, a voice for the dumb."[12]

One of the prominent Christian leaders of our time, Bishop Desmond Tutu, was a powerful force in the Truth and Reconciliation Commission in South Africa, which involved an earnest quest to tell the truth about abuses in the apartheid system and to seek national healing and reconciliation. Though it was often portrayed in secularist terms, the Truth and Reconciliation Commission drew on deep Christian resources in the South African culture and was based on the biblical promise "You shall know the truth, and the truth shall set you free." Tutu was praised for his efforts, but his constant testimony that confession and repentance can lead to forgiveness stirred up harsh criticism as well. As one critic put it, "You would think that by the time one had gotten to be Tutu's age, he would have learned how to hate a little more. But there is this problem with Desmond. He actually believes the gospel." God is present. God remembers the poor and oppressed. God offers healing and forgiveness. God summons the whole creation toward a new and hopeful future. These are the words we hear in worship, and these are the words we offer in testimony to the world.

James Billington, the librarian of Congress and a student of Russian history, heard all of these words of testimony in a few remarkable days he spent in Moscow in 1991. He happened to be in Moscow in August of that year, during the time when the old Soviet regime was giving way to a new social order. These were tense and dangerous days, and power was balanced on a razor's edge. Boris Yeltsin and a small group of defenders occupied the Russian White House and successfully managed to face off an enormous number of tanks and troops poised to attack, to put down the rebellion, and to restore the old guard in the Soviet Union.

Surprisingly, a key role in this successful resistance was played, said Billington, by the *babushkas,* the "old women in the church," and their courageous public Christian witness. These kerchiefed old women, who had kept the Orthodox Christian church alive during the Communist period, were the butts of many jokes told over the years by Russians and Westerners alike. Nothing could have seemed more pathetic or irrelevant than they, and they were widely regarded as evidence that religion was close to death in the Soviet Union.

And yet on the critical night of August 20, 1991, when martial law was proclaimed and people were told to go to their homes, many of these women disobeyed and went immediately to the place of confrontation. Some of them fed the resisters in a public display of support. Others staffed medical stations, others prayed for a miracle, while still others, astoundingly, climbed up onto the tanks, peered through the slits at the crew-cut men inside, and told them that there were new orders, these from God: Thou shalt not kill. The young men stopped the tanks. "The attack," said Billington, "never came, and by dawn of the third day we realized that the tide had turned."[13]

In skirmishes leading up to these critical days, three young defenders of the White House had been killed. As their funeral procession wound through the streets of Moscow and passed in front of the White House, Boris Yeltsin himself emerged to speak to the parents of the three young men. What he said to them was strikingly significant. "Forgive me, your President, that I was unable to defend and save your sons," he said. "Forgive me," Billington observed, is what one Russian customarily says to those next to him at the Lord's table before taking communion. In a time of public grief, Yeltsin was reciting the familiar language of worship and "was assuming responsibility in a society where none in power had ever accepted responsibility for anything."[14]

A STARTLING AND REFRESHING WORD

Talking about our faith in public and political settings is not an easy thing to do. It requires courage and a willingness to go against the grain. No one should minimize the costs or the risks of doing this. When Jesus spoke openly about God's presence, God's claim on human life, God's way of living, and God's hope, those who heard him rose up and killed him.

Similarly, when Christian people get out there in the public arena and speak the truth in love, some entrenched power is almost always threatened, and this testimony can be ignored, resisted, rejected, or reviled. Sometimes—and this may be the worst fate of all—Christian testimony is not rejected overtly but is resisted instead by being turned inside out and idolatrously made to serve that which is not God. Christian-sounding language can be whipped into line and forced to march to the drumbeat of racism, greed, tyranny, or crass nationalism.

But even though Jesus was rejected and crucified for what he said, his words also brought people to life. There were those who heard him gladly and hung their hopes on his every word. And so it is with Christian witness today. Sometimes it so startles a world jaded by lies and seductions that the very truthfulness of it comes as a deep refreshment.

Not long ago, the university where I teach awarded several honorary degrees at the commencement service. Each of the recipients was introduced, was given a diploma and a citation, and then made a short speech.

University students are not well known for their decorum during graduation exercises, and this one was no exception. A Pulitzer Prize–winning playwright received a degree, and the students chatted noisily and joked throughout his speech. The same was true for the world-class mathematician and the internationally known diplomat.

In fact, there was only one moment during the entire ceremony when the students were silent and attentive. It was when a man named Hugh Thompson was speaking. Thompson was probably the least educated man on the platform that day. He grew up in the little village of Stone Mountain, Georgia, in a family of modest means. He started but did not finish college, choosing instead to enlist in the Army, where he became a helicopter pilot.

On March 16, 1968, he was flying a routine patrol in Vietnam when he happened to fly over the village of My Lai just as American troops, under the command of Lieutenant William Calley, were slaughtering dozens of unarmed and helpless villagers—old men, women, and children. Thompson set his helicopter down between the troops and the remaining Vietnamese civilians. He ordered his tail gunner to train the helicopter guns on the American soldiers, and he ordered the troops to stop killing the villagers. He then called for other helicopters to come to the area and to evacuate the surviving villagers and take them to hospitals.

Hugh Thompson's actions saved the lives of dozens of people. However, for his efforts, he was almost court-martialed by the Army. It was thirty years before the Army recognized him as a hero and awarded him the Soldier's Medal for his courage.

As he stood at the microphone, the normally rowdy student body grew still. "I'd like to thank my mother and father for trying to instill in me the difference between right and wrong," Thompson said to the hushed crowd. "We were country people, born and raised in Stone Mountain, but they taught me 'Do unto others as you would have them do unto you.' . . . just a little thing called the Golden Rule; you try to live by it, and you'll be OK."[15]

The words were simple, but the students were startled and invigorated by them. In a world of weasel words, self-serving words, lying words, they were amazed at these words, words of Jesus, words from Sunday school, words from worship, words of Christian testimony, words that could enable a man to put a helicopter down in the

The Six O'Clock News

middle of an atrocity and to do the right thing. The leapt to their feet in a standing ovation, the only one of the day.

Hugh Thompson was courageous in Vietnam, but perhaps no more courageous than that day, when he stood out in the public square and gave his testimony.

Chapter 8

WHISPERED SECRETS AND BEDTIME PRAYERS

At the end of the day, when the sun has gone down and the cool evening breezes begin to blow and the fever of the day's busyness subsides, the moment for reflection comes. The evening shadows become the deep blue of night, the hum of street and market wanes, the television is at last turned off, cell phones are silenced, the time for sleep approaches, and our minds wander over the events of the day. Was this a good day? Did I live joyfully this day? Were the hours well spent? Were my deeds well done? Were my words well spoken?

The coming of the night is not only a time for summing up this one day but also a reminder of our mortality. The dying of the day's light is a symbol of the truth that our light will some day flicker and fail and we will ourselves pass into the evening shadows. As for human beings, says the psalmist, "their days are like grass; they flourish like a flower of the field, for the wind passes over it, and it is gone, and its place knows it no more" (Psalm 103:15–16). We sense the truth of the psalmist's wisdom in our hearts. We have spent the day talking in a thousand ways—chatting over coffee, calling neighbors on the phone, giving lectures in the classroom, working out a problem with coworkers, laughing with friends at lunch, swapping small talk on the bus, exchanging information with customers, confessing our love, comforting and disciplining our children, praying, singing, complaining, telling jokes—but at night, as we turn down the covers on the bed and prepare to sleep, we are at least dimly aware that a time is coming when our voices will be silenced and our words heard no more.

In the glare of the sun, our words seem endless, but they are not. It seems that we could just go on talking and talking, that if we say something foolish, cruel, or stupid today, there will always be a tomorrow to set the record straight and to say it better, smarter, and kinder. But at night we know that our words, like our days, are numbered, and our voices are heard for only a brief span, then silence. Our prayer at night is, Teach us, O Lord, to count our days and to count our words as well. Teach us how to speak wisely and well. Teach us, O Lord, to tell the truth in love, to tell the truth so that the love of God and the love of neighbor grow.

In the quiet reflection of night, we acknowledge, if we are honest with ourselves, that not all of the words we have spoken this day have been wise, true, or kind. The New Testament letter of James warns us that our speech can do great good but also great harm. The tongue, says James, can sing praises to God but can at the same time destroy other people, who are made in God's image. The tongue is not very large, James says, but it can be full of deadly poison (James 3:5–12).

Like every other human being, I know that this is true from personal experience. Not long ago, I was having a conversation with my daughter about her experiences growing up. My daughter is a bright and strong woman, the mother of two children, and we were talking about how, as a parent, she sees now in her children many of the struggles, fears, accomplishments, and joys she remembers from her own childhood. The conversation was good and it was honest, and at one point my daughter remembered an argument we had when she was a teenager. What it was we were arguing about we have both long forgotten, but my daughter vividly remembers one moment of this dispute. Evidently we were exchanging sharp words, father and daughter locked in battle, and I threw up my hands in frustration and said, "You're nothing but trouble to me!"

It was a stupid thing to say. It is the kind of thing people say to each other, even people who love each other, in the heat of an argu-

144

TESTIMONY

ment, but it was a dumb thing to say nevertheless. And it wasn't true, either. Like most parents, I cherish my children deeply, and my daughter and my son are the apples of my eye, my treasures, and a great joy to me. It was simply never even remotely true that she was nothing but trouble to me. I have never once really thought that, and in fact, I don't remember saying it.

But she does. It was years, she said, before she could think about that moment without pain. For me, my words were just hurled into the heated atmosphere, soon to evaporate, but for her, those words, hastily spoken, were shaped like poison darts, and they found their target in her heart.

Teach us, O Lord, how to count our words. Here in the night, when the fire burns low and we think about the day and pray, teach us how to speak wisely.

A TIME TO SPEAK, A TIME TO KEEP SILENT

Part of wisdom in learning how to speak as Christians is not only knowing when to speak but also knowing when to keep our mouths shut. I have repeatedly described the role of Christian testimony as telling the truth, the whole truth, and nothing but the truth, but there are also times when Christians have no right to speak, even to speak the truth, times when faithful testimony means faithful silence.

Take gossip, for instance. Gossip is sometimes true. It may be factually true that the woman who lives across the street is having an affair or that one of our golfing partners has a serious drinking problem or that a high school girl in town slipped away recently to a clinic for an abortion. What is more, whispering about this to confidants may be very satisfying, pleasurable, even almost irresistible. After all, gossip is juicily interesting, and spreading it gives us a rare surge of moral or ethical superiority. We may even be able to clothe our gossip in the language of noble motives. We are "concerned about Alice" or "morally offended by Sean's behavior" or, we tell the listening party, "I normally wouldn't breathe a word of this, but I think you deserve to know what's going on." Prayer groups even get in on the gossip, sharing damaging information about people "so we can lift them up more fully in prayer."

But even if we are telling the truth in our gossip and even if we can find the motives to justify it, the fact remains that gossip usually hurts people more than it helps them. As I have said, Christian testimony is not just telling the bare-knuckled truth. It is telling the truth in order to increase the love of God and neighbor. Most gossip decreases our regard for the neighbor.

As noted in Chapter Two, the theologian Dietrich Bonhoeffer formulated a rule for his community that no Christian should speak about another person behind that person's back, even when the intent is to help and to do good. All talk about other people, he said, should be done out in the open, in their hearing. This is a stern rule, and we learned that the people in Bonhoeffer's community, try as they might, finally could not keep it.

We probably would not be able to keep Bonhoeffer's rule either, but the purpose of the rule is worth noting nevertheless. When we are about to tell a sensitive piece of information about someone else, perhaps we should turn the tables in our imagination. What if the gossip we are about to tell about someone else were true not about that person but about us, and the other person was about to reveal it? Would we think of this as a loving thing or a hurtful thing? Would we be helped by the revelation or betrayed by it? Would telling this increase the love of God and neighbor or not?

Gossip is just one aspect of a much larger and very complex issue about the keeping and telling of secrets. Sissela Bok, who was an ethicist at Harvard University, wrote a whole book about the ethics of secrets,[1] and she makes the valid point that just because a person wants something kept secret does not necessarily mean that this secrecy is a good thing. A parent who is abusing a child, a city official who is embezzling funds, or an airplane pilot who has a serious heart condition may not want this known, but the welfare of others depends on the truth being brought into the open. Sometimes people do not have the right to keep even very sensitive and personal information secret.

On the other hand, Bok says, having and keeping some secrets is essential to human identity and well-being. Only a totalitarian government would use cameras to watch our every move and allow no secrets. People who keep private diaries may well be able to express and work through problems and emotions in the writing of the journal that would not be possible if they knew other people would be pawing through the pages. Even in our most intimate relationships, it would be a violation of our selves if we had to blurt out every thought and feeling and could have nothing kept back.

In describing the relationship between secrecy, in a positive sense, and personal identity, Bok says:

> Control over secrecy provides a safety valve for individuals in the midst of communal life—some influence over transactions between the world of personal experience and the world shared with others. With no control over such exchanges, human beings would be unable to exercise choice about their lives. To restrain some secrets and to allow others freer play; to keep some hidden and to let others be known; to offer knowledge to some but not to all comers; to give and receive confidences and to guess at far more: these efforts at control permeate all human contact.
>
> Those who lose all control over these relations cannot flourish in either the personal or the shared world, nor retain their sanity.[2]

Christians would agree with this basic idea; people have a need to keep some secrets and not to keep others, and likewise, some truths should be told openly and others kept quiet. But Christians would add one important claim to the mix, namely, that secrets are temporary and only the truth finally endures. Secrecy may be a good thing, but only in the short run. In the long run and in the ultimate end of things, the truth will come out. Almost all keeping of secrets, even of the most necessary secrets, is connected to fear, the fear that if the truth came out, damage would be done. Christians look for the time when perfect love will finally cast out all fear, and hence Christians

Whispered Secrets and Bedtime Prayers

view secrets like they do locks on doors or guns on the belts of police: devices that are temporarily necessary because of human sin and brokenness but ultimately destined for obsolescence.

One of the classic Christian prayers says, "Almighty God, unto whom all hearts are open and all desires known, and from whom no secrets are hid, cleanse the thoughts of our hearts by the inspiration of thy Holy Spirit, that we may perfectly love thee and worthily magnify thy holy name." Notice particularly the phrase "no secrets are hid" from God. Now, the picture of a God who knows all our secrets may strike us as creepy, even terrifying, a God who peers through keyholes and reads our mail, a ruthlessly scrutinizing God who, like a judgmental Santa, knows when you've been sleeping, knows when you're awake, and knows when you've been bad or good. But Christians do not say this prayer fearfully; they say it confidently and hopefully, because the God we have met in Jesus Christ is "merciful and gracious, slow to anger and abounding in steadfast love" (Psalm 103:8). In relationship to this God, the truth will finally not hurt us; indeed, we desire to be fully known by this God, whom we trust. In Christ "the truth will make you free" (John 8:32), and there is finally no reason to fear, no reason to keep secrets.

So if the truth will ultimately not hurt us and will in fact set us free, why should we ever keep secrets? Why not just pull the veil back now on as many secrets as possible? Why isn't every form of the truth—even gossip, even betrayed secrets—a good thing? Again, Sissela Bok helps us see why when she observes that the whole reason people have secrets in the first place is to protect things that are sacred, intimate, and fragile and to maintain boundaries around that which is dangerous or forbidden.

Let's take these one at a time and begin with the sacred. If a person has had a powerful religious experience, some deep meeting with holy mystery, whether this involves the birth of a child, a sudden moment of clarity, or a vision in the night, there are some things that can be said about it, but there are some parts of it that are ineffable, at least for the time being. If this person can say nothing at all about the experience, it will soon be lost, even to the one who had it. On the other hand, every encounter with the mystery of God involves depths that cannot

148

TESTIMONY

yet come to expression. Indeed, a person who talks immediately and excessively about a so-called profound religious experience, a person who is converted on Tuesday and writes a book about it on Thursday, raises questions about the true depth of the experience. We are promised that eventually our relationship to God will come to full and rich expression in praise, but for the moment, real encounters with God involve dimensions too deep to bring immediately into language. If it is a truly sacred experience, something of it must remain for the moment in secrecy.

Something similar is true for intimacy. Lovers want to be known—hunger to be fully known—to each other, but the growth toward intimacy takes place over time. To reveal too little is to fear the intimacy, but to reveal too much, too soon, is to run the risk of being absorbed or dominated by the other. So lovers engage in a dance of revelation and concealment, desiring to be transparent to the beloved but at the same time holding something back, protecting the self that desires to love and to be loved.

In regard to fragility, sometimes the truth is a heavy weight, and it requires more strength than we have in the present to bear it. A surgeon who must tell a patient that the surgery revealed cancer throughout the body may well hold back the information for a while, waiting for the patient to regain enough physical and emotional strength to hear the awful news. A new employee at a company may someday choose to share with her coworkers her struggles with clinical depression once she has grown to trust them, but she would cringe in humiliation if this were posted on the office bulletin board her first day at work. Or who among us would wish to know the terrible truth of the date and hour of our death? We are too fragile in our mortality for that. We fear that it would not be a freeing truth but a morbid and paralyzing sentence of doom.

So it is with dangerous or forbidden knowledge. Posting on the Internet information about how to make a nuclear bomb or the address of a facility where battered women have fled to be safe may involve truth, but wisdom would keep such knowledge secret. Children will eventually learn that their parents are sexual beings, but to bring a small child into the bedroom during lovemaking is to transgress a crucial boundary.

So Christians know that we bow before a God "before whom no secrets are hid" and that ultimately the truth is to be embraced fully and without fear. But as we make our way "East of Eden" in a broken world, we must make moral choices about if and when we speak. Sometimes we tell secrets, and sometimes we keep them. There will be ambiguities and hard choices, but the goal is clear: our testimony is always to increase the love of God and neighbor.

OUT OF THE MOUTHS OF INFANTS

As the darkness falls and the day becomes night, we also begin to reflect on those who will come after us, on the generations to follow after we are gone. Especially we wonder whether our own children will share our faith and be able to give testimony of their own.

Nathaniel Volf was barely two years old when he asked his father the biggest question a person, regardless of age, can ask. "Daddy," said Nathaniel, "what God mean?" Nathaniel's father is Miroslav Volf, an internationally recognized theologian, but that did not help him with his son's question. "I was taken aback," he admitted, but he recovered quickly and began to do his best to tell Nathaniel about the God who created the sky, the seas, the land, the birds, the fish, and all the other animals.[3]

However, Miroslav Volf was not satisfied with his answer. "I sensed," he said, "that I was talking past him and felt humiliated as a theologian (though I am not sure that one could answer this question in any way that a two-year-old would understand)." When he told a friend about his frustration, she reassured him that in such matters, what you say to a child is not nearly so important as what you do. Volf thought about his friend's advice and finally decided that she was only partly right. What we do matters, Volf agreed, but so do words.

What led Volf to this conclusion was his memory about how words had mattered in the passing on of faith in his own life. Volf's father, born in Europe to a Catholic father and a Baptist mother, abandoned his Christian faith when he was a teenager. During World War II, Volf's father was a prisoner in a concentration camp, and the horror of the camp only intensified his loss of faith. If God existed and could permit such suffering, this God "deserved to be cursed and spat upon."

But then his father came to know another prisoner in the camp, a man who was as hungry as the rest of the prisoners, who bore daily the same humiliations and cruel labor, but whose eyes sparkled with life, whose hands were unwearied in helping others, and whose words were full of his faith in Jesus Christ and in a God whose love was powerfully present even in the hell of the camp. "Gradually," said Miroslav Volf, "my father started believing this strange man," and from then until his dying day, his father's Christian faith was strong and unwavering.

Miroslav, however, passed through his own phase of rebellion against God. His father, once agnostic, was steadfast, but now it was Miroslav's turn to reject the faith. However, if his father's faith had been renewed by words, so was Miroslav's. "When I was brought back to faith," he said, "it was through the prayers of my devout mother. Every evening when her prodigal son would go out, she would wait on her knees for him to return."

Now Miroslav Volf prays, too, that his own son Nathaniel will find his way to a deep and lasting Christian faith. "I want him to embrace Christianity as a faith by which to live and for which to die," Volf says. How will this happen? Volf knows that deeds matter; how he acts as a person of faith will deeply influence his son, but Volf also remembers his father's encounter with the man at the concentration camp and his mother's prayers, and he knows that words count, too. "Right language about God matters," he says, but finally all parental talk and action can take root only by the grace of God. "If the seed sown by word and deed is to grow and bear fruit," Volf says, "it will need the life-giving water of God's Spirit."[4]

Two comforting lessons can be drawn from Miroslav Volf's story. The first is that even a renowned theologian finds it difficult to speak of faith with his children. Children ask questions about God that are difficult, even impossible, to answer, and even when we imagine that we have some wisdom to share, the right words are hard to find. The second comforting insight, however, is that our faithful words do count. Even words that come from uncertain knowledge, even words about faith that are stammered out, help form faith in our children.

Brad Wigger is a Christian educator who has spent much energy thinking about how the Christian faith gets communicated and taught in families. But he readily admits that all parents, even clergy parents, feel on thin ice when speaking to their children about faith.

In his book *The Power of God at Home,* Wigger tells about a remarkable exchange he had some years ago with his own son, David. Shortly after the Wiggers had moved across town to a new apartment, Brad was putting the then three-year-old David to bed, and David was saying his bedtime prayers. He prayed mostly the usual—a blessing for his friends, family, pets, and stuffed animals—but then David ended the prayer with something unexpected. "And God," he said, "I miss you."

Brad's jaw dropped. David *misses* God? What does this mean? Why does my son miss God? Like most parents in such a circumstance, Brad was not sure what to do, what to say. He wanted to reassure his son that God was still present, or at least tell his son a soothing story, but he was not sure this would be helpful. So instead he said nothing, tucked his son into bed, and went and told his wife about David's prayer so that both of them could worry about their son missing God.

The next morning, over breakfast, Wigger decided to bring the matter up very gently with his son:

> "David, last night when you were praying, you said you missed God."
>
> "Oh yeah," he answered, "but that's okay now."
>
> "What do you mean?"
>
> "Well," he said, "God came to me last night."
>
> I interrupted. "David, you mean like in a dream?" (My modern brain had to find some way to explain this.)
>
> "I dunno, I guess. Anyway, I was playin' in the sandbox behind our old house, and God came and said, 'Come David,' so I followed, and we came here and now God is here with us in our new home!"[5]

Here again we see that the key is not knowing just what to say or possessing all knowledge about the Christian faith. The key is to provide the kind of environment in the home where talking about God can take place. If talking about God is as expected and as natural as talking about playmates or television programs, children will learn to ask questions about God, speak their thoughts about God, and come to trust this God, whose presence is woven into the fabric of the everyday.

In a church in a distant city, I once encountered a child, a little girl, who had obviously benefited from a home where talk about God was a part of the everyday round of conversation, and it showed in her maturing faith. She only said one thing in my presence, but it was one of the most profound theological insights I have ever heard.

I had published a brief article in a religious magazine in which I made a passionate argument that children should be present every week in the regular services of Christian worship (rather than packed off to be baby-sat or to go to some segregated "junior church" service). I further argued that if children were present in worship, changes would have to be made to account for their presence and to make worship truly intergenerational.

Not long after the article appeared, my telephone rang, and a woman who identified herself as the Christian educator in a certain congregation filled the receiver with compliments on my article.

"Thank you," I replied, glowing in her praise.

"But there's just one thing," she said. "We're still not quite sure what this would look like in actual practice, and we'd like for you to come to our church and show us how to do it."

My brow grew moist. "Hey, look," I protested, "I was just writing an article."

"Right," she said, "but we'd still like you to come and show us how this works in practical terms."

What could I do? I went to this church, and I did the best I could to model in practice the sort of intergenerational worship I had written about in theory. With the help of the Christian educator, we planned what promised to be a wonderful service to be held in the fellowship hall of the church on Sunday afternoon. Families were to be seated at tables stocked with flour, water, and yeast. Adults and children would mix the ingredients into bread dough, and while they were kneading it for baking, they would talk with each other about their faith. Then the dough would be taken to the adjacent kitchen to be baked, and while the aroma of baking bread wafted through the fellowship hall, I would preach an intergenerationally apt sermon, followed by the Lord's Supper using the bread that the families had made. It was a lovely plan.

It was a disaster. A hard rain started early that Sunday morning, and by the time families arrived for the afternoon service, children had been unhappily cooped up inside all day. Families were in a surly mood, the children were rambunctious, and the dough-kneading exercise threatened to get out of control. Vexed children were crying, chairs were being knocked over, wearied parents were getting testy, and some of the older children were throwing wads of wet dough across the room. Clouds of flour dust filled the room.

Then there was a breakdown in the kitchen. The ovens were painfully slow, and the bread took an eternity to bake. I padded the sermon, which dragged on and on. When we finally arrived at the end of this misguided adventure, the room was cacophonous. Parents were yelling, babies were crying, children were screaming. For the finale, the script called for me to raise my hands over this uproar and to give a blessing: "The peace of Christ be with you all." The word *peace* seemed a mockery in this chaos, but I was too tired and distracted to think of anything more fitting, so I just said it. "The peace of Christ be with you all."

And then a miracle occurred. Out of the tumult came this child's voice. When I said, "The peace of Christ be with you all," somewhere out there in the clamor she simply said, "It already is." That's all she said, "It already is," but the power of it made me shiver. A systematic theologian would speak of the proleptic presence of God's reign, how God's ultimate victory, which eventually all creation will see, is experienced by believers even now. But this little girl said it better. In the middle of a room in uproar—or maybe even in the middle of a world in uproar—she already knew the peace of Christ. And she said so.

LET THE WORDS OF MY MOUTH
BE ACCEPTABLE ...

At the end of the day, in the quiet of honest reflection, we know that we have sinned. We know that not all that we have said this day has been good or pure or kind or faithful. We are human beings, and our words are broken and stained. We have not told the whole truth and we have not always spoken with grace and we have not always built up the love of God and neighbor.

Jesus said, "I tell you, on the day of judgment you will have to give an account of every careless word you utter; for by your words you will be justified, and by your words you will be condemned" (Matthew 12:36). Such a teaching would be too heavy to bear, and none of us could withstand it, were it not for the fact that this same Jesus said, "Come to me, all you that are weary and carrying heavy burdens, and I will give you rest. Take my yoke upon you, and learn from me; for I am gentle and humble in heart, and you will find rest for your souls . . . for my yoke is easy, and my burden is light" (Matthew 12:28–30).

Our words matter. Our words are a main pathway on which our faith goes forth into the world. Others know us by our words, and God gives us words to tell the truth in love and to provide testimony to the world of who we are and what we believe. But our words are gathered up into the true Word, our lives gathered up into the true Life, and our testimony gathered up into the true Witness, Jesus Christ. Therefore, our words and our lives float on a sea of mercy and forgiveness. This grace does not make us careless with our words. It rather calls us at night to prayers of repentance and confession and sends us out the next day to speak as children of forgiveness and hope. Our words, then, are a burden and a yoke placed on us by Jesus, but because of his mercy, his yoke is easy and his burden is light.

A PARTING BLESSING

In the night, as we move toward sleep and rest from the labors of the day, we could hardly do better than to pray the famous prayer of Cardinal Newman:

Whispered Secrets and Bedtime Prayers

O Lord, support us all the day long of this troublous life,
until the shadows lengthen and evening comes,
and the busy world is hushed,
and the fever of life is over, and our work is done.
Then, in your mercy, grant us a safe lodging
and a holy rest and peace at last. Amen.

This prayer acknowledges that God has been with us through the day, and through all our days, and prays for God to give us safety and peace in the night and at the end. In terms of testimony, we might think of the prayer this way: the God who has been in our mouths and in our speaking through the day will speak words of blessing to us at the end of the journey: "Well done, good and faithful servant."

Sometimes our own word of blessing to another participates in this divine blessing. My friend Thomas Lynch is a poet, a prize-winning essayist, and a funeral director. The literary gifts are his own, but the mortician's craft he learned from his father, a funeral director before him. Thomas told me that one of the things that most impressed him about his father was that when he would prepare the dead for burial, he would talk to them. Before he closed the casket, he would take one last look and say things like "Norman, my good friend, you did a good job." When his own wife died, he closed the casket and said with deep sadness, "Rosie, Rosie, how can I live without you?" When he himself died, Thomas and his brothers closed the casket saying, "You were the best, the best." Well done, good and faithful servants.

Angelo Roncalli was an Italian peasant who rose to become Pope John XXIII, one of the most beloved figures in Christian history. During his service as pope, the Roman Catholic Church underwent the major upheaval known as Vatican II, a tumultuous and controversial time of reform and change. It is said that in the midst of this volatile time, Pope John would read his bedtime devotions, say his private prayers, and then, before turning out the light, would say to himself, "But who governs the church? You or the Holy Spirit? Very well, then. Go to sleep, Angelo, go to sleep."[6]

Here is the testimony: We are all floating in a sea of mercy and grace and providence. So go to sleep. In confidence and trust, go to sleep.

Epilogue

A LAST WORD

> There was this East Indian Jesuit named Tony de Mello who used to
> tell this story about disciples gathered around their master, asking
> him endless questions about God. And the master said that anything
> we say about God is just words, because God is unknowable. One dis-
> ciple asked, "Then why do you speak of him at all?" and the master
> replied, "Why does the bird sing? She sings not because she has a
> statement but because she has a song."
>
> —ANNE LAMOTT, *Operating Instructions*[1]

Some years ago, I found myself at a dinner party at which one of the
guests was a prominent church leader from a former Iron Curtain
country. The Soviet Union had collapsed a few years before, and Eastern European countries were then beginning to put democratic reforms into place.

We peppered our guest with questions about what church life
had been like in the Soviet era, and he answered them with candor
and unaccustomed freedom. He spoke encouragingly of the vibrant
faith and courageous commitment of the Christians in his land, but
he also described the fears of years of being watched and under sus-
picion in a controlled society.

"KGB-type agents infiltrated the church," he said. "We would
go to church meetings and know that some of the pastors present
were really agents posing as clergy, listening to what we said, report-
ing everything. There were spies in our midst."

"Spies? Posing as clergy?" a man at the table said.

"Yes," he replied, "but of course, we knew who they were."

"Knew who they were?" the same man said with surprise. "I thought they were secret agents."

"Oh, they were, but we could tell," he replied. "There was something in their voice that gave them away."

Something in their voice. I have thought many times since about what he said, and I recognize the truth of his observation. There is something about people's voices that reveals the truth about them. I mean the kind of thing that speech-activated lie detectors pick up, but I mean more, too. I mean what Jesus was talking about when he said that he was the Good Shepherd and that his sheep know his voice (John 10:4, 11). A voice discloses the essence of a person, and what a person says, how a person says it, and the very sound of the voice are all revealing of the truth.

But now that I have come to the end of this book and have tried to imagine how Christians talk in the world from sunrise to the close of day, I wonder if the world knows us by the sound of our voices. If spies and secret agents can infiltrate society on behalf of control and fear, I am praying that Christians can infiltrate the world for faith, grace, and hope. If we do, then the world will say, "We could tell who they were. We knew. There was something in their voice that gave them away."

Notes

Foreword

1 Later in life, Augustine drew on all the honesty and literary art he could muster in writing a moving autobiography that has been known across the centuries as *The Confessions.* A historian has recently declared that a more fitting title for this book would be *The Testimony* (Garry Wills, *Saint Augustine* [New York: Viking-Penguin, 1999]). Words as "precious cups of meaning" comes from *The Confessions* I.16, words as "weapons" comes from *The Confessions* XI.2.

Acknowledgments

1. Ben Cheever, quoted in Sam Roberts, "On Acknowledgments, the Inquisition Was Easier," *New York Times,* November 27, 2003, p. E1.
2. Ibid., p. E1.

Chapter One

1. Lynna Williams, "Personal Testimony," in Kay Cattarulla, ed., *Texas Bound: 19 Texas Stories* (Dallas, Tex.: Southern Methodist University Press, 1994), pp. 191–204.
2. Edgar Guest, "Sermons We See," in *Collected Poems* (Cutchogue, N.Y.: Buccaneer Books, 1996), p. 599.

3. I am indebted to John McClure of Vanderbilt University, who once described a congregation as "talking itself into being Christian" and who inspired my variation on the phrase. See John S. McClure, *The Roundtable Pulpit: Where Leadership and Preaching Meet* (Nashville, Tenn.: Abingdon Press, 1995), p. 50.

4. C. Frederick Buechner, "What Will You Be?" *Princeton Seminary Bulletin,* New Series, 1984, 5(3), 192.

5. Richard K. Fenn, *Liturgies and Trials: The Secularization of Religious Language* (New York: Pilgrim Press, 1982), pp. 122–123.

6. Alexander Solzhenitsyn, "A World Split Apart," address given at Harvard University, June 8, 1978.

7. Helen Prejean, "With a Human Being Who's About to Be Killed," *Peacework,* April 2000, p. 6.

8. Elaine Pagels, "Introduction," in Thieh Nhat Hanh, *Living Buddha, Living Christ* (New York: Riverhead Books, 1995), p. xiii.

9. The Westminster Larger Catechism of the Reformed tradition has the following as the first question and answer: "Q. What is the chief and highest end of man? A. Man's chief and highest end is to glorify God and fully to enjoy him forever."

Chapter Two

1. Deborah Griffin Bly, "Go Tallit on the Mountain," *Books and Religion,* Spring 1992, p. 3. The incident is also recorded in Milton J. Coalter, "The Craft of Christ's Imperfect Tailors," *Theology Today,* October 1993, pp. 387–396.

2. Bly, "Go Tallit," p. 4.

3. Martin Marty as quoted in "Testimony," a sermon preached by the Reverend Fred A. Niedner Jr. at the Chapel of the Resurrection, Valparaiso University, March 15, 1999.

4. Craig Dykstra, *Growing in the Life of Faith: Education and Christian Practices* (Louisville, Ky.: Geneva Press, 1999), p. 119.

5. Paul Tillich, "The Power of Love," in *The New Being* (New York: Scribner, 1955), pp. 27–28.

6. Reynolds Price, *A Palpable God* (New York: Atheneum, 1978), p. 14.

7. See Heidi Neumark, *Breathing Space* (Boston: Beacon Press, 2003),

pp. 9–10. The account of this event appeared in Thomas G. Long, "The Dream Church" in *Exploring and Proclaiming the Apostles' Creed* (Grand Rapids, Mich.: Eerdmans, 2004), pp. 238–239.

8. C. S. Lewis, *Reflections on the Psalms* (New York: Harcourt Brace, 1958), p. 94.

9. Thomas G. Long, "When Half-Spent Was the Night," *Journal for Preachers,* Easter 1999, pp. 19–20.

10. Eberhard Bethge, *Dietrich Bonhoeffer: A Biography* (Minneapolis, Minn.: Fortress Press, 2000), p. 428.

11. From *The Rule of St. Benedict,* chap. 6, "The Spirit of Silence."

Chapter Three

1. Throughout this chapter, I use "Sunday" and "Sunday morning," naming the time of Christian worship, strictly for simplicity and clarity. What I wish to do is to draw both contrasts and connections between "worship time" (whether that be on Sunday, Saturday, or another day) and the mundane time of the workaday world.

2. William H. Willimon, *The Service of God: Christian Work and Worship* (Nashville, Tenn.: Abingdon Press, 1983), p. 52.

3. Richard Lischer, *Open Secrets: A Spiritual Journey Through a Country Church* (New York: Doubleday, 2001), p. 81.

4. Thomas Merton, *Conjectures of a Guilty Bystander* (Garden City, N.Y.: Image Books, 1968), pp. 156–157.

5. Theodore J. Wardlaw, "A Holy Soundtrack," *The Weekly* (published by Central Presbyterian Church, Atlanta), April 8, 2000, p. 1.

6. See the analysis of this psalm in Michael Fishbane, *Biblical Text and Texture: A Literary Reading of Selected Biblical Texts* (Oxford: One World Publications, 1998), pp. 84–90.

7. Kathleen Norris, "Words and the Word," *Christian Century,* April 16, 1997, p. 381.

8. George Bernard Shaw and Alan Jay Lerner, *Pygmalion and My Fair Lady* (New York: New American Library, 1994), p. 169.

9. Dykstra, *Growing in the Life of Faith,* p. 119.

10. Stephen L. Carter, *The Culture of Disbelief: How American Law and Politics Trivialize Religious Devotion* (New York: Basic Books, 1993),

pp. 204–206. My thanks to the Reverend Elizabeth McGregor Simmons for alerting me to this section of Carter's book.

11. Flannery O'Conner, "A Temple of the Holy Ghost" in *The Complete Stories* (New York: Farrar, Straus & Giroux, 1979), p. 238.

12. Diane M. Komp, *A Window to Heaven: When Children See Life in Death* (Grand Rapids, Mich.: Zondervan, 1992), pp. 28–29.

13. Donald McCullough, *Truman* (New York: Simon & Schuster, 1992), p. 984.

14. Rebecca Chopp, "Theology and the Poetics of Testimony," *Criterion,* Winter 1998, p. 2.

15. Janet Malcolm, *In the Freud Archives* (New York: Knopf, 1984), pp. 70–71.

16. Julius Novick, "Mr. Williams and the Crazy Lady," *The Village Voice*, December 27, 1976, pp. 73–74. Thanks to Patrick Willson for pointing me to this story.

Chapter Four

1. Thomas Merton, "First and Last Thoughts," in Thomas E. McDonnell, ed., *A Thomas Merton Reader* (New York: Harcourt Brace, 1974), p. 18.

2. Thomas Merton, "Day of a Stranger," in Lawrence S. Cunningham, ed., *Thomas Merton, Spiritual Master* (Mahwah, N.J.: Paulist Press, 1994), p. 215.

3. James Weldon Johnson, *God's Trombones: Seven Negro Sermons in Verse* (New York: Viking Press, 1938), p. 17.

4. C. Frederick Buechner, *The Alphabet of Grace* (New York: Seabury Press, 1970), pp. 21–22.

5. Sören Kierkegaard, quoted in George Appleton, ed., *The Oxford Book of Prayer* (Oxford: Oxford University Press, 1985), p. 98.

6. Anne Lamott, *Traveling Mercies* (New York: Pantheon Books, 1999), p. 82.

7. John Calvin, *The Institutes of the Christian Religion,* bk. 3, ch. 20.

8. Jim Forest, "Dorothy Day," in Michael Glazier and Thomas J. Shelley, eds., *The Encyclopedia of American Catholic History* (Collegeville, Minn.: Liturgical Press, 1991), p. 415.

9. Robert Ellsberg, quoted in Gerry McCarthy, "The Social Edge Interview: Author Robert Ellsberg," *The Social Edge.Com: A Monthly Social Justice and Faith Magazine,* November 2003 [http://www.thesocialedge.com].

10. Forest, "Dorothy Day," p. 414.

11. Buechner, *Alphabet of Grace,* p. 38.

12. Hubertus Halbfas, *Theory of Catechetics: Language and Experience in Religious Education* (New York: Herder & Herder, 1971), p. 136.

13. Peter L. Berger, *A Rumor of Angels: Modern Society and the Rediscovery of the Supernatural* (Garden City, N.Y.: Doubleday Anchor, 1970), p. 55.

14. Ibid., p. 56.

15. Erik H. Erikson, *Childhood and Society,* 2nd ed. (New York: Norton, 1963), p. 269.

16. Berger, *Rumor of Angels,* p. 57.

17. Paul Tillich, "You Are Accepted," in *The Shaking of the Foundations* (New York: Scribner, 1962), p. 162.

18. David Bartlett, *What's Good About This News?: Preaching from the Gospels and Galatians* (Louisville, Ky.: Westminster/John Knox, 2003), p. 17.

19. Mary Ann Bird, quoted in Leonard Sweet, *Strong in the Broken Places: A Theological Reverie on the Ministry of George Everett Ross* (Akron, Ohio: University of Akron Press, 1995), p. 93.

20. Forest, "Dorothy Day," p. 414.

21. William J. Boyd, personal correspondence.

Chapter Five

1. William Diehl, *The Monday Connection* (San Francisco: HarperSanFrancisco, 1991), pp. 64–66.

2. C.A.J. Coady, *Testimony: A Philosophical Study* (Oxford: Clarendon Press, 1992), pp. 6–7.

3. Carlyle Marney, quoted in William H. Willimon, *Sighing for Eden: Sin, Evil, and the Christian Faith* (Nashville, Tenn.: Abingdon Press, 1985), p. 24.

4. Don Flow, "A Business Owner's Mission: Working as a Christian in a Car Sales Firm," in Robert Banks, ed., *Faith Goes to Work: Reflections from the Marketplace* (Eugene, Ore.: Wipf & Stock, 1993), p. 75.

5. Ibid.

6. Peter J. Gomes, *The Good Book: Reading the Bible with Mind and Heart* (New York: Morrow, 1996), pp. 197–198.

7. Ibid., p. 198.

8. Walker Percy, *The Message in the Bottle: How Queer Man Is, How Queer Language Is, and What One Has to Do with the Other* (New York: Farrar, Straus & Giroux, 2000), p. 138.

9. Ibid., p. 139.

10. Bartholomew Sullivan, "Bowers Convicted of Killing Dahmer. Ex-Klan Leader Gets Life Term in '66 Murder," (Memphis) *Commercial Appeal,* August 22, 1998.

11. Ibid.

12. Sandra Herron, "Reflecting Christ in the Banking Industry: The Manager as Prophet, Priest, and King," in Banks, *Faith Goes to Work,* p. 88.

13. Ibid., p. 84.

Chapter Six

1. James A. Sanders, *God Has a Story Too: Sermons in Context* (Philadelphia: Fortress, 1979), p. v.

2. Michael Frost, *Seeing God in the Ordinary: A Theology of the Everyday* (Peabody, Mass.: Hendrickson, 2000), p. 15.

3. Though I am applying it to another context, much of what I say about speaking the faith as a gift was inspired by an address given by Dr. John R. Claypool at the Candler School of Theology on September 17, 2003.

4. Henri J. M. Nouwen, *Reaching Out: The Three Movements of the Spiritual Life* (Garden City, N.Y.: Doubleday, 1975), p. 51.

5. Dan Wakefield, "Returning to Church," *New York Times Magazine,* December 22, 1985, p. 24.

6. Ibid., p. 28.

7. Ibid.

8. Ibid.

9. Hans Kung, *On Being a Christian* (Garden City, N.Y.: Doubleday, 1976), p. 20.

10. Renata Adler, quoted in David McCullough, *People, Books, and Book People* (New York: Harmony Books, 1981), p. 1.

11. Thornton Wilder's image of the tapestry is described in Harold Kushner, *When Bad Things Happen to Good People* (Boston: Hill, 1982), pp. 25–26.

12. Eudora Welty, *One Writer's Beginning* (Cambridge, Mass.: Harvard University Press, 1984), p. 90.

13. These words are often attributed to C. S. Lewis. See, for example, Robert E. Kennedy, *Zen Spirit, Christian Spirit: The Place of Zen in Christian Life* (New York: Continuum, 1995, 1995), p. 59.

14. John Updike, *More Matter: Essays and Criticism* (New York: Knopf, 1999), p. 851.

15. I am grateful to Chaplain Dale McAbee for this story.

Chapter Seven

1. From a cartoon by Robert Mankoff in the *New Yorker,* January 6, 1997.

2. Stephen L. Carter, *The Culture of Disbelief: How American Law and Politics Trivialize Religious Devotion* (New York: Anchor Books, 1994), pp. 4, 6, 279.

3. Ibid., p. 3.

4. Walter Brueggemann, *Biblical Perspectives on Evangelism: Living in a Three-Storied Universe* (Nashville, Tenn.: Abingdon Press, 1993), p. 129.

5. Peter J. Gomes, *The Good Book: Reading the Bible with Mind and Heart* (New York: Morrow, 1996), p. 179.

6. Daniel Berrigan, *The Trial of the Catonsville Nine* (Boston: Beacon Press, 1970), p. 83.

7. Lillian Daniel, "Minute Fifty-Four," in Jackson W. Carroll and Carol E. Lytch, eds., *What Is Good Ministry? Resources to Launch a Discussion: A Collection of Portraits and Essays About Good Ministry* (Durham, N.C.: Duke Divinity School, 2003), p. 7.

8. Ibid.

9. Ibid.

10. John Lewis, *Walking with the Wind: A Memoir of the Movement* (New York: Simon & Schuster, 1998), p. 501.

11. Mary Munford, "The Television Journalist: Telling and Doing the Truth as a Way of Glorifying God in the Media," in Banks, *Faith Goes to Work,* p. 51.

12. Rowan Williams, "Remembering for the Future," in *A Ray of Darkness: Sermons and Reflections* (Cambridge, Mass.: Cowley, 1995), p. 209.

13. James H. Billington, "The Religious Dimensions of Post-Modern Change," American Theological Library Association, Summary of Proceedings, 52/1998, pp. 154–155. The account of the *babushkas* is taken from this essay and from comments made in various addresses by Billington.

14. Ibid., p. 155.

15. Hugh Thompson as quoted in Emory [University] Report, May 28, 2002, n.p.

Chapter Eight

1. Sissela Bok, *Secrets: On the Ethics of Concealment and Revelation* (New York: Vintage Books, 1983).

2. Ibid., p. 20.

3. Mirsolav Volf, "Faith Matters," *Christian Century,* April 4, 2001, p. 24.

4. Ibid.

5. Brad Wigger, *The Power of God at Home: Nurturing Our Children in Love and Grace* (San Francisco: Jossey-Bass, 2003), pp. 23–24.

6. Peter Nichols, *Politics of the Vatican* (New York: Praeger, 1968), p. 109.

Epilogue

1. Anne Lamott, *Operating Instructions: A Journal of My Son's First Year* (New York: Fawcett Columbine, 1993), pp. 180–181.

The Author

Thomas G. Long is the Bandy Professor of Preaching at Emory University's Candler School of Theology in Atlanta, Georgia. He lectures in universities and churches around the world, and he has written books on preaching, communication, worship, and biblical studies. He was named in *Newsweek* as "one of the twelve most effective preachers in the English-speaking world."

Index

Crucifixion, 140
Cry for Mercy: Prayers from the Genesee (Nouwen), 121
Culture, faith testimony in conflict with. *See* Countercultural messages
Culture of Disbelief, The (Carter), 55, 130

D

Dahmer, E., 103
Dahmer, V., 102, 103
Daniel, L., 135–137
Dawn, promise in, 69–70. *See also* New day
Day, D., 81, 87, 108
de Mello, T., 157
Dead Man Walking movie, 15
Death row inmates, caring for, ministry of, 15–16
Deception: outright, using words to avoid, 95; susceptibility to, 91–94
Decision making, basis of, 93
Defense mechanisms, 92
Democratic National Convention, 11–12
Diehl, W., 89–90
Discipline, 36, 37, 78
Divine blessing, 156
Doolittle, E., 52
Double vision of other people, 45–46
Doubts, 116, 118, 121, 122
Dying: preparing for, 18; truth in, 33–34. *See also* Mortality
Dykstra, C., 23–24, 55

E

Easter, 30, 31, 113, 127
Ecstatic sounds, 52, 53
Erickson, E., 84
Ethics of secrets, 146–147
Eucharist, 17, 60
Evangelism, 5, 132
Evangelists, 8
Eve, 94–95, 96
Everyday life: bearing witness to the truth in, 58–64; connections between worship and, 39–43, 73; dependence of, on belief in truth-telling, 92–93; gifts of, teaching about, 111; obligations of, 70; presence of God woven into, 153; rehearsal for, 42–43, 54–55, 73; religious language in, 82–83; soundtrack for, 47–49; truth-telling in, 96–97; view from, 125; words from, as rehearsal for worship, 57. *See also* Workday life
Evidence/proof, 114–115
Expectant silence, 53
Experience: learning through, 31, 32; sacred, and secrecy, 148–149

F

Failure, wisdom from, 34–35
Faith language. *See* Religious language
Faithful silence, knowing time for, 145–150
Faithful witness, 29, 30, 86
False witness, 28
Faulty witness, 61
Fear: absence of, 84, 148, 150; of being alone, 118; internal, of public speaking about faith, 132; and secrecy, 147–148
Feet, beautiful, 113
Fiddler on the Roof musical, 79
Finkenwald seminary, rule at, 34–35
Flow, D., 97
Focus in prayer, 78
Forgetting of self, 72
Forgiveness: accepting responsibility and, 139–140; sin and, 60–62, 90, 137–138, 155
Fragility and secrecy, 148, 149
Fragments of testimony, 123, 124–128
Frame of reference, 42
Freedom: gift of, 120–121; in the truth, 148
"From a Distance" song, 113
Frost, M., 113

G

Garden of Eden, 79, 94–95, 96, 118
Gathering for worship, 44–47
Genesis, 53, 75, 77, 94
Genesis 1:26, 104
Genesis 1:28, 75
Genesis 3:1, 95
Genesis 12:1, 15
Gift of freedom, 120–121
Gift-giving speech, 118–120
Glossolalia, 52
God: action of, 75; call of, 73, 75, 77, 82; conversation with, 53–54; grace of, 48; message from, Jesus as, 54, 60, 113; in the midst of life, 20; people of, 63, 64, 102, 103, 104; presence of, 127, 128, 135, 138, 153; a story told by, life as, 126; trust in, 84; the Word of, 15, 75, 76; work of, 73, 74
God chatter, 8–10, 22
God Has a Story, Too (Sanders), 112
God talk: authentic, 8, 10, 11, 12–13, 23–24, 90; ceremonial, 9, 10, 12–13; harmful, 113–114; offensive, 22–23
"God willing" phrase, 9–10
God's Trombones (Johnson), 76
Golden Rule, 141
Gomes, P., 98–99, 132–133
Good Friday hymn, 47
Good news, people who bring, 113
Gossip, 34, 145–146
Grace, 48, 97, 111, 156
Greenspan, A., 129
Growing in Faith (Dykstra), 55
Guest, E., 4

H

Halbfas, H., 82
Half-truths, 95–96
Harmful God talk, 113–114
Harmful words, speaking, 144–145
Harvard University, 13–14
Hebrews 1:1, 54
Herron, S., 105–107

Holy Spirit, finding the, 127–128
Holy Week passion play reenactment, 30–31
Homeless shelter, 81
Hospitality, 57, 120–122
Huckleberry Finn (Twain), 16
Human worth and work, 62–64
Humility in prayer, 78–79
Hymns: and everyday life, 47–48, 60; goal in, 57; meaning of, 53. *See also* Worship

I

Identity, personal: as people of God, 63, 64; and secrecy, relationship between, 147
Idolatry, 24
In the Freud Archives (Malcolm), 62
Inner urges, expressing, 9
Insults, comedian, effect of, 101–102
Integration, public school, 102–103, 134
Integrity, 84, 97
Interfaith boundaries, concern over, 22
Intergenerational worship, 153–154
Intimacy and secrecy, 148, 149
Invitation to lunch, meaning of, 109
Irenaeus, 19
Isaiah, 15, 28–29
Isaiah 43:10, 29
Israelites, 124

J

James 2:1, 8-9, 107
James 3:5–12, 144
Jeremiah, 14
Jesus: on anxiety, 132–133; and baptism, 124; on behavior, 90; being asked about, example of, 21–22; claiming proof of, issue of, 114–115; on the commandments, 101; on the day of judgment, 155; demeanor of, 104–105; on God's work, 73; on his sheep, 158; learning by, 31–32; living life patterned after, 19; and the loaves and the fishes, 123; as a message from

God, 54, 60, 113; parables of, 20; in passion play reenactment, 30–31; peace of, 80; on prayer, 78; on public proclamation, 135; quoting, and context, issue of, 129; rejection and crucifixion of, 140; relationship to, 17, 18; on self-absorption, 72; simple words of, 141; song about, and his love for children, 111; speaking truth about, 11; stories of, telling, passing on, 115; trust in, 118; on the very first Easter, 113; as witness, 29–30, 155

John, 11, 14
John 1:1, 14, 65
John 1:14, 97
John 6:1–14, 123
John 8:1–11, 90
John 8:32, 148
John 9:4, 73
John 10:4, 158
John 10:11, 158
John XXIII, Pope, 156
Johnson, J. W., 76
Jordan River, 124
Journalists, responsibility of, for truth-telling, 137
Journey, continual, life of faith as a, 15, 16
Joyfulness, 70–74
Judgment day, 155

K

Key witness, 29–30
Kierkegaard, S., 78
King, M.L.K., Jr., 137
King, M.L.K., Sr., 11–12
Knowledge: basis of, 93; with experience, 32
Komp, D., 58
Ku Klux Klan, 102
Kung, H., 124

L

Lamott, A., 78, 157
Language: power of, 84; varied uses of,

19. *See also* Religious language
Language school, 32–33, 34, 38, 47, 54–57, 62, 103
Learning: by Jesus, 31–32; in worship, 104–108
Learning environment, 32–33, 34, 35, 37–38
Lewinsky, M., 96
Lewis, C. S., 33, 126
Lewis, J., 137
Libya, bombing raid against, view of, 26–27
Life as a story, 126
Lincoln, A., 129–130
Lischer, R., 43
Lord's Supper, 57, 60, 80, 154
Louisiana State Penitentiary, 15
Love: creating, by putting into words, 6; expression of, 105–106, 112, 144
Luke 2:40, 32
Luke 9:24, 72
Lunch, conversation over, 108, 109–128
Luther, M., 78, 123
Lutheran Church of the Holy Spirit, 107
Lying: appearance of, in reassurances to children, 83–84; in court, 28; discomfort with, 5; reasons for, 62. *See also* Deception
Lynch, T., 156

M

Magazines, 8
Maguire, D., 64
Malcolm, J., 62
Mark 10:21, 105
Mark, Gospel of, 104–105
Marketplace pressures, 97
Marney, C., 94
Marty, M., 23
Matthew 6:7, 78
Matthew 10:16, 90
Matthew 10:27, 135
Matthew 12:28–30, 155
Matthew 12:36, 155
Matthew 16:18, 118

Roman Catholic Church, reform of, 156

Roman Catholic Mass, traditional, 65

Romans 10:15, 15, 113

Romans 10:17, 110

Roncalli, A., 156

Russia, communist. *See* Communist Russia

179

Practicing Our Faith:
A Way of Life for a Searching People

Dorothy C. Bass

Paper

ISBN: 0–7879–3883–1

As wise as grandparents, a good guide to living within our families and communities with integrity and generosity.
—Kathleen Norris, author of *Dakota* and *The Cloister Walk*

Many Christians are looking for ways to deepen their relationship with God by practicing their faith in everyday life. Some go on retreats but are often disappointed to find that the integrated life they experienced in a place apart is difficult to recreate in their day-to-day world. Many thoughtful, educated Christians search for spiritual guidance in Eastern religious traditions, unaware of the great riches within their own heritage.

To all these seekers, *Practicing Our Faith* offers help that is rooted in Christian faith and tradition. The contributors examine twelve central Christian practices—such as keeping Sabbath, honoring the body and forgiving one another—by placing each in historical and biblical context, reexamining relevance to our times, and showing how each gives depth and meaning to daily life. Shaped by the Christian community over the centuries yet richly grounded in the experiences of living communities today, these practices show us how Christian spiritual disciplines can become an integral part of how we live each day.

DOROTHY C. BASS is a noted church historian and director of the Valparaiso Project on the Education and Formation of People in Faith. She lives with her husband and children in Valparaiso, Indiana.

A Song to Sing, A Life to Live:
Reflections on Music as Spiritual Practice

Don Saliers, Emily Saliers

Hardcover

ISBN: 0–7879–6717–3

The Indigo Girl and her father focus on the many dimensions of music in one's spiritual life.
—*Publishers Weekly,* February 9, 2004

Indigo Girl Emily Saliers and her father Don Saliers explore the many dimensions of music as it relates to our spiritual lives. Music is a central practice in most expressions of spirituality and faith—whether it's the Christian music of seeker services, traditional hymnody, liturgical chant and singing, or popular music ballads about the meaning of life. In this rich exploration of music across all these settings and styles, authors Don and Emily Saliers interweave their own stories as well as those of others to reveal the importance of music as spiritual practice and a force for good in our lives, looking at such topics as music and justice, music and grief, music and delight, and music and hope.

DON SALIERS is professor of theology at Candler School of Theology at Emory University. EMILY SALIERS is a member of the Indigo Girls, an award-winning folk-rock duo known for their social activism. Don and Emily both live in Atlanta, Georgia.